TORCH BIBLE COMMENTARIES

THE GOSPEL ACCORDING TO
SAINT MARK

THE GOSPEL ACCORDING TO

SAINT MARK

A. M. HUNTER

SCM PRESS LTD

334 01040 3

First published 1949
by SCM Press Ltd
58 Bloomsbury Street, London WC1
Thirteenth impression 1978

Printed in Great Britain by
Fletcher & Son Ltd, Norwich

CONTENTS

Gospel Verse
No.   *Page*

viii

ix

x

xi

xii

PREFACE

The day of the aridly critical commentary is past. Nowadays the demand is for a 'theological' commentary, i.e. a commentary which, while satisfying all the requirements of scientific scholarship, lays the chief emphasis on the religious and theological meaning of the sacred text. It is a salutary change of emphasis, and I hope that my little book will help to meet this demand. It is based on the Authorised Version and is meant for the general reader.

In preparing it for the press I have consulted all the standard English commentators—Swete, Menzies, Rawlinson, Blunt, Turner, etc.—but I have derived most stimulus from Dr. Walter Lowrie's *Jesus according to St. Mark*, a book not well known in this country, but replete with theological insight.

My warm thanks are due to three persons: first, to the Rev. Anderson Nicol, M.A., Minister of West St. Nicholas, Aberdeen, who found time in a busy ministry to type the MS. and supply some very useful comments; and, second, to two other friends who enriched the MS. with their criticisms—the Rev. A. D. Alexander, B.D., lecturer in Biblical Criticism in Aberdeen University, and one of my own students, Mr. George B. C. Sangster, D.S.C., B.D.

King's College,
Aberdeen.

December 1947.

A. M. HUNTER.

BIBLIOGRAPHY

BENGEL. *Gnomon Novi Testamenti*

C. H. TURNER. *St. Mark* (S.P.C.K.)

A. W. F. BLUNT. *St. Mark* (Clarendon Bible, O.U.P.)

A. E. J. RAWLINSON. *St. Mark* (Westminster Commentaries, Methuen)

VINCENT TAYLOR. *The Gospel according to St. Mark* (Macmillan)

T. W. MANSON. *The Beginning of the Gospel* (O.U.P.)

WALTER LOWRIE. *Jesus according to St. Mark* (Longmans)

D. S. CAIRNS. *The Faith that Rebels* (SCM Press)

ALAN RICHARDSON. *The Miracle Stories of the Gospels* (SCM Press)

J. JEREMIAS. *The Parables of Jesus* (SCM Press)

INTRODUCTION

In order to read a book of the New Testament intelligently, we must know, if possible, who wrote it, when, why, and for whom it was written. Happily we are in a position to answer these questions in the case of Mark with tolerable certainty. But before we come to them, we must say something concerning

THE GOSPEL BEFORE THE GOSPELS

Gospel, a fine old English word which means 'God story' or 'good story', translates the Greek word *euangelion*.

Originally, *euangelion* meant the reward given to a man who brought good news. Then it came to mean the good news itself. Then—and this is the New Testament sense—it came to signify the Good News proclaimed by and centring in Jesus Christ. Later still, it came to be applied to canonical 'memoirs' of Jesus. With this last usage we reach the common usage of to-day. By the Gospels we mean written records of the Good News which came into the world with the coming of Christ.

But the Good News was being proclaimed in the world long before there was any written record of it. In the first generation of Christians (roughly A.D. 30-60) there was no written Gospel, but there was a *kerygma*. This Greek word means 'a preached message', and thanks to the labours of modern scholars we are now able to form an idea of its contents.

A careful comparison of the early speeches in Acts (see particularly Acts 10. 36-43) with certain passages in Paul's letters where clearly he is handling traditional material (see particularly 1 Cor. 15. 3 ff.) yields a common outline of the message which formed the earliest version of the Good News. It ran as follows:

God's promises made to his people in the Old Testament are now fulfilled.

The long-expected Messiah, born of David's line, has come.

He is Jesus of Nazareth, who went about doing good and wrought mighty works by God's power; was crucified according to the purpose of God; was raised by God from the dead and exalted to his right hand;

He will come again for judgment.

Therefore let all who hear this message repent and be baptised for the forgiveness of their sins.

This was the outline. Of course it must have been filled in by the earliest preachers with stories about Jesus. Of these there was no lack, for many still lived who had seen and heard Jesus; and in all the centres of early Christianity— Jerusalem, Antioch, Caesarea and Rome—there must have grown up cycles of stories about Jesus which the 'saints' passed from one to the other and which the apostolic preachers used to illustrate their sermons.

But what about the teaching of Jesus? The *kerygma* evidently said little about that. Yet we should err if we supposed that the early Christians completely forgot the memorable sayings of him who spake as never man spake. On the contrary, we know that they treasured up these sayings for the guidance they supplied for Christian life and practice. St. Paul, for example, could quote 'words of Jesus' to settle hard questions in his churches (see e.g. 1 Cor. 7. 10, 11. 23 ff., and Acts 20. 35). And by and by a collection of these sayings was compiled to act as a guide to Christian behaviour for those who had become Christians. (Note that this collection of sayings was used by Matthew and Luke in the composition of their Gospels. Nowadays it is commonly referred to as Q.)

So the materials later to be woven into our Gospels took shape during the generation that followed the Crucifixion and Resurrection. This is the period of *the oral tradition*— the period when men still preferred the living voice of eye-witnesses to any written record of Jesus. But the time was to come when men were to feel the need for a written record.

This brief summary of 'the Gospel before the Gospels' paves the way for an appreciation of Mark's achievement. He was (in Mr. Laurence Housman's words):

> The saint who first found grace to pen
> The life which was the Life of men.[1]

But before we come to his work, let us ask what were the causes that moved the early Church to desire a written record of Jesus Christ and the Gospel.

A generation had gone past since Jesus had died and risen: a generation in which 'the hallowed fire' of the Gospel had flown from Jerusalem to Rome. Many of the eyewitnesses had now 'fallen asleep'; others had been killed. It became increasingly important that the facts about Jesus should be set down before the time should come when there would be nobody left able to say, 'I remember Jesus Christ as a man.' Besides, converts were flocking into the young churches: converts who needed instruction in the Christian Faith, who wanted to know more about him whom they called Lord and Master. In short, the need was felt for a written record of the Lord Jesus, and with the need came the man.

That man was Mark. He it was who wrote the earliest Gospel. What materials lay to his hand? To begin with, he had an outline of the Lord's ministry in the *kerygma*—a rough and ready outline, to be sure, but one that could be filled out with stories about Jesus. As we shall see, he had probably his own memories of Jesus during the Last Week in Jerusalem; he had many more stories he had got from his friend Peter; and, since he lived and moved in circles where many more stories about Jesus were current, he was obviously a man well qualified for his task. So, somewhere

[1] *Songs of Praise*, No. 228.

in the sixth decade of the first century, and in the city of Rome, Mark procured a reed-pen and papyrus and sat down to compose the earliest Gospel.

THE AUTHOR

But how do we know that the author of the earliest Gospel was Mark?

The answer, very briefly, is that all tradition declares Mark to have been the author, and that there is no reason why he should have been so unanimously named unless the tradition were true.

Here are three samples of the tradition. Our earliest bit of tradition goes back to Papias, a Christian writer who lived in the first half of the second century. This is what he says:

> Mark, having become the interpreter of Peter, wrote down accurately everything that he remembered, without however recording in order what was said or done by Christ.

Some time between A.D. 160 and 180, the man who wrote the so-called *Anti-Marcionite Prologues to the Gospels* testified as follows:

> Mark, who was called stump-fingered because his fingers were small by comparison with the rest of his body, was Peter's interpreter, and after Peter's decease wrote down this same Gospel in the region of Italy.

Finally, Irenaeus about A.D. 180 put on record:

> After their deaths (i.e. Peter's and Paul's) Mark, the disciple and interpreter of Peter, himself also gave us a written record of the things preached by Peter.

Where the tradition is so unanimous we need have not the slightest hesitation in ascribing the Gospel to Mark, about whom, happily, we know quite a lot.

He has been called the best-known of the secondary
characters in the apostolic age. His Hebrew name was John;
but, since then, as now, there were many Johns, he is usually
known by his Latin name Marcus. The son of Mary who
was hostess to the Mother Church in Jerusalem in its earliest
days (Acts 12. 12), he was, if Mark 14. 51 refers to himself
(see the notes), a friend of Jesus during at least the last week
of his ministry, and it is not unlikely that it was one of the
rooms in his home which was the scene of the Last Supper.
We have surer information about him some years later.
Acts tell us that he accompanied Paul and Barnabas (who
was his cousin, Col. 4. 10) on the First Missionary Tour
(Acts 13. 5, 13) as their 'assistant'. Because Mark deserted
them at Perga and went home, Paul refused to have him at
the start of the Second Missionary Journey, and the two
apostles quarrelled. That quarrel, however, must have been
composed, for less than ten years later Mark shared Paul's
imprisonment in Rome (Col. 4. 10-12; Philem. 24. and cf.
2 Tim. 4. 11).

But Mark is linked in history not with Paul only, but with
Peter. In the first Epistle of Peter, v. 13, the writer tenderly
calls him 'Mark, my son'—a phrase which must imply a
disparity in age between the two men of some fifteen to
twenty years, as it clearly proves the affection which sub-
sisted between them. Moreover, as we have seen above, the
tradition of the Church is that Mark acted as Peter's interpreter and later used the materials so gathered in the composition of his Gospel. What 'interpreter' means is not
certain. Did Mark help Peter with his Greek? Or did he
assist him to turn his Greek into Latin? Or does the word
mean quite generally 'private secretary'?

The important thing, however, is this clear testimony to
the close connection between Mark's Gospel and Peter's
preaching. While we may not claim that all the material in
Mark's Gospel came to him from Peter and therefore reflects
the testimony of an eyewitness, we shall not go far astray if
we find in the Gospel according to St Mark the 'reminis-
cences of Jesus as told by Peter to his friend John Mark'.

PLACE OF WRITING

Where did Mark write his Gospel? This question is by implication answered already. Not only does tradition say that it was written 'in the region of Italy', but, as we have seen, there is New Testament evidence that Mark was with both Paul and Peter in Rome. The contents of the Gospel bear out the view that the Gospel was written in Rome. A study of the Epistle to the Romans demonstrates that the Church in Rome was predominantly Gentile, and Mark clearly writes with Gentile readers in view. Not only does he use a great many transliterated Latin words like *centurio*, *speculator*, *legio*, *denarius*, etc., but he is at great pains to explain Jewish customs and ways of life for the benefit of his readers (7. 3 f.; 14. 12; and 15. 42). Finally, he quotes the actual Aramaic words which Jesus used on certain occasions, as e.g. *Talitha cumi*, *Ephphatha*, and *Abba*, but he always carefully translates them for readers who presumably had no Semitic languages.

DATE

Irenaeus says that it was after the deaths of Peter and Paul that Mark wrote his Gospel. Now Peter and Paul were martyred during the Neronian persecution which followed the great fire in Rome in A.D. 64. On the other hand, the Gospel seems to have been written before the Fall of Jerusalem in A.D. 70. This we infer from Mark 13. 14 (cf. Luke 21. 20), which, by its reference to the expected appearance of Antichrist, suggests that the troubles had already begun. Some time, then, between 65 and 70 are the narrow limits within which we may date the Gospel. The readers whom he had primarily in view were no doubt the Christians in Rome who were then going through a time of bitter suffering and persecution. They would be heartened to read in Mark's Gospel that their suffering was not unforeseen and unexpected, for Jesus their Lord had not only predicted tribulation for his disciples, but had himself drained the cup of suffering to the dregs for their redemption.

THE CONTENTS OF MARK

The Gospel falls into five parts:

1. Prologue: before the Ministry   1. 1-13
2. The Galilean Ministry   1. 14—8. 26
3. The journey to Jerusalem   8. 27—10. 52
4. Jerusalem: Death and Resurrection   11—16. 8
5. Epilogue (by another hand)   16. 9-20

1. The Prologue occupies the first thirteen verses. In fulfilment of Old Testament prophecy, John the Baptiser appears in the wilderness down near the Dead Sea, calling Israel to repent and announcing the near advent of the Messiah. The great day dawns and Jesus comes down from Nazareth in Galilee and is baptised by John in Jordan. A divine voice tells him that he is the Son of God, and he retires into the desert, where he is tempted by the devil.

2. At 1. 14 the first main section of the Gospel begins. After the Baptist's arrest, Jesus comes into Galilee with the startling announcement that the decisive hour has struck and that God's Reign is beginning. Let men 'turn' again to God and make this Good News their own. He calls two pairs of brothers from their fishing-nets to be his disciples, and, entering Capernaum, begins to heal and preach. His fame runs like a kindling flame through Galilee. But his claim to forgive sins, his consorting with the 'down-and-outs', his radiant religion, offend the religious leaders; and by and by he is compelled to teach and heal his growing mass of followers by the Lake of Galilee. Twelve men (the nucleus of the new People of God, i.e. the Church) are appointed to form an inner circle and to serve as his lieutenants in the work of the Kingdom. His enemies accuse him of being in league with the powers of evil, and some declare him mad. The Galilean ministry proceeds: he teaches the multitude about God's Reign in parables and manifests its presence by his mighty works. The Twelve, having been to school with him, are now sent forth in pairs to tell men about God's Reign and to gather in God's people. When they

return, the Galilean ministry reaches its climax in a great mass-feeding of five thousand people.

Thereafter Jesus leads the Twelve north-west into the heathen regions of Tyre and Sidon; and on their return journey, at Caesarea Philippi, almost in the shadow of snow-capped Hermon, a decisive stage is reached. Peter, in answer to Jesus' leading question, confesses Jesus to be the Messiah, the heaven-sent Saviour for whom the Jews had been waiting for centuries. At once Jesus tells his disciples that he must go to his throne by way of a cross. The Twelve are shocked and incredulous. From that time on the shadow of a cross falls ever more darkly across the story.

3. The next section—the journey to Jerusalem—extends from 8. 27 to 10. 52. Six days after Peter's confession, Jesus is transfigured on a mountain top before three of his disciples. Henceforward the whole story moves towards Jerusalem. Passing through Galilee to Capernaum, he travels south, through Perea, till he reaches Jericho. And as he goes, we see him healing demoniacs and blind men, blessing little children, answering the Pharisees, and all the while preparing his disciples for the cross. From Jericho he ascends to Bethany, two miles from Jerusalem.

4. The last main section, which begins at 11. 1 and ends at 16. 8, relates what befell in Jerusalem: it describes the Passion, the Crucifixion, and its shining sequel.

There follow all the events which we associate with Holy Week: the Triumphal Entry and the Cleansing of the Temple; the teaching in the Temple courts and the Anointing at Bethany. Finally, on the Thursday night, he holds the Last Supper in an upper room in Jerusalem, endures the Agony in Gethsemane, is arrested, tried and condemned. On Friday morning, at 9 a.m., he is lifted up on a cross, and at 3 p.m. he dies. Some hours later Joseph of Arimathea, with the consent of Pilate the Roman Governor, buries Jesus' body in a rock tomb. It is Friday evening and the story of Jesus seems at an end.

But no; there is an amazing sequel. On the Sunday morning (as we should say) some women going to anoint Jesus' body, find the grave empty, and a mysterious 'young man' declares: 'He is not here; he is risen.' Awe-stricken, the women flee from the tomb. . . .

5. The Epilogue. At 16. 8 the authentic text of Mark's Gospel breaks off abruptly with the words "For they were afraid . . .' The Epilogue, 16. 9-20, is by another and later hand. (Did Mark mean to end his Gospel at this point? Or was he interrupted? Or, likeliest of all, was the last sheet of the papyrus-roll accidentally torn off?) It tells how the risen Jesus appeared to his disciples and commanded them to preach the Gospel to all creation.

THE CHARACTERISTICS OF THE GOSPEL

The first characteristic is the rough vigour and vividness of Mark's style. Mark is not a trained man of letters—indeed, he often writes clumsily, inelegantly, ungrammatically—but he is one of those people who instinctively tell a story well. The purist in language may criticise him for many faults—his heaping-up of participial clauses, his excessive use of the word 'straightway' (Greek, *euthus*, forty-one times), his manifold redundancies; but no man may gainsay his vigorous descriptive style. He has an action story to tell, and he tells it vividly, adopting with effect, for example, the historic present tense (151 examples) which lends a graphic colour to his tale. His pages, too, are sprinkled with self-authenticating little vividnesses which suggest the presence of an eyewitness like Peter behind his narrative. Thus, to choose a few examples, it is Mark who lets us see the five thousand squatting down upon 'the green grass' like so many 'garden plots', each of them holding fifty or a hundred people (6. 39 f.); as it is Mark who gives us four unforgettable pictures of Jesus: first, asleep on 'the rower's cushion' in the fishing boat during the storm (4. 38); next, taking the little children 'in the crook of his arms' (10. 16); then looking with real affection on a rich young man (10. 21); and finally, striding on ahead of his disciples, a great lonely figure wholly absorbed in his Passion, as he travels the road to Jerusalem (10. 32).

When we turn from form to content, the first thing that

strikes us is Mark's realism. No other evangelist is so 'familiar' in his references to Jesus. No other evangelist dwells so often on his human emotions. Now Jesus is grieved and sighs deeply in his spirit (7. 34; 8. 12); now he is moved with pity (6. 34); now he 'marvels' at the unbelief of his fellow countrymen (6. 6); now he grows 'indignant' at the conduct of his disciples (10. 14). Once he looked round 'with anger' on his critics (3. 5, see notes); on another occasion he was seized with 'deadly fear' (14. 33 f.). The careful reader may multiply such references. For Mark shows us one who is bone of our bone, flesh of our flesh; one who is touched with the feeling of our infirmities; one who sorrows even unto death; in short, a real man like us in all respects save one—sin. 'When God would save man,' said Jeremy Taylor, 'he did it by way of a man.' Mark never lets us forget this, and we are grateful for it.

But if we were to stop here, the half would not have been told. If Mark never lets us forget that Jesus was a man, he is equally sure that he is the Son of God. That note is struck in the very first words—'The beginning of the Gospel of Jesus Christ the Son of God.' It recurs again and again in the Gospel. Artless though Mark's Christology may be, there is no doubt that he believes Jesus to be supernatural and divine. It is not only true that a divine voice at the Baptism and again at the Transfiguration proclaims him to be such (1. 11 and 9. 7), or that Jesus himself makes the same stupendous claim (12. 6; 13. 32; and 14. 62); through the whole story there runs 'a mysterious undercurrent' which (as C. H. Dodd says) reminds us that the story is more than that of a martyrdom. There is a mystery about this man. He speaks as one directly inspired by God (1. 22). He possesses powers which evoke from those who behold them feelings of unutterable awe (2. 12; 4. 41; and 6. 50). He is conscious that he is doing a work for 'the many', i.e. for the common deliverance, which he alone can do (10. 45). He speaks of his death as inaugurating a new era of relations between God and man (14. 24). For the story that Mark tells is not simply of 'one more unfortunate gone to his death', nor even of one more prophet or reformer sealing his testimony to the truth, as God gives him to see it, with his life-blood. It is the story of how God's Kingdom—his redeeming rule—was once and for all time manifested in his only Son, Jesus Christ, and realised 'with power' by the Resurrection.

For sheer beauty of narrative we shall go to the Gospel according to St. Luke. For profound insight into the ultimate meaning of the Gospel we shall prefer St. John. For a systematic presentation of Christ's teaching we shall choose St. Matthew. But for the earliest, simplest, and shortest record of 'the strong Son of God' who 'was manifested' (as the collect finely phrases it) 'that he might destroy the works of the devil and make us the sons of God and heirs of eternal life', there is but one book—the Gospel according to John Mark.

NOTE ON Q

In the commentary the reader will note frequent references to Q. For the benefit of those who have not studied what is called 'the Synoptic Problem', let me say that Q is the symbol used by scholars to denote the sayings-source which both St. Matthew and St. Luke used in the compilation of their Gospels. See my book, *Introducing the New Testament* (S.C.M. Press), Chapter V.

O Almighty God, who hast instructed thy holy Church with the heavenly doctrine of thy Evangelist Saint Mark: Give us grace, that, being not like children carried away with every blast of vain doctrine, we may be established in the truth of thy holy Gospel; through Jesus Christ our Lord. Amen.

(The Collect for St. Mark's Day
in the BOOK OF COMMON PRAYER)

I

THE FORERUNNER

I. 1-8
(MATT. 3. 1-12; LUKE 3. 1-18)

How differently the four evangelists ring up the curtain on the drama of redemption! Matthew begins with an elaborate genealogy. Luke, as becomes a literary man, prefaces his Gospel with some polished 'prolegomena'. John, like the eagle which is his emblem, soars at once into the theological empyrean and makes the finest beginning in literature. Mark, who was no *littérateur*, though he could tell a story uncommonly well, puts down half a dozen blunt, important words by way of superscription and forthwith plunges into nis narrative.

1. The beginning of the Gospel of Jesus Christ the Son of God
Some take this to be the title of the whole book, as though the story of the Ministry, Death, and Resurrection were only the beginning (cf. Acts 1. 1, 'All that Jesus began to do and teach'). This is possible, for in a true sense Acts is the story of the acts of Christ continued. But it is improbable that Mark had this in mind when he wrote his superscription. He was thinking rather of John the Baptist's mission as the beginning of the Gospel. (Cf. Acts 10. 36 f. 'The word . . . beginning from Galilee after the baptism which John preached.')

GOSPEL, of course, means Good News, God's Good News. But is it the Gospel which Jesus preached, or the Gospel about Jesus—the Gospel that he was, and is? Probably we ought not to try to choose between those meanings here, for in Mark's view, as in Dr. Dale's, Jesus came not only to preach the Gospel, but that there might be a Gospel to preach. JESUS is the Greek form of Joshua, as CHRIST is the Greek equivalent of the Hebrew Messiah, the Anointed One, the Saviour for whom the Jews had been waiting for centuries, the one in whom all God's purposes of redemption are focused and consummated, the bearer of God's kingdom to men. At first a title, it is here a proper name. If the words 'the Son of God', which are not found in some MSS., are a later addition, they are just such words as Mark might himself have written; for it is 'the strong Son of God' whom he will portray again and again in his pages. But they are probably genuine.[1]

After the superscription, Mark launches *in medias res*. Prophecy had said that the Messiah and the Day of the Lord would be preceded by a forerunner; and it was in accordance with this prophecy that John the Baptist appeared in the grim and houseless region down near the Dead Sea.

2. As it is written in the prophets

It was a cardinal point in the preaching of the first apostles that the Gospel story was a real fulfilment of the promises and prophecies of the Old Testament. Mark makes that point in vv. 2-3. But the A.V. rather obscures it. What we have in the Greek is a protasis and apodosis, thus: 'As it is written in prophecy . . . so John appeared,' etc. The true reading here is, however, not 'in the prophets' but 'in Isaiah the prophet' (R.V.). Mark has made a slight slip; for it is only the second quotation that comes from Isaiah (40. 3); the first is from Mal. 3. 1.

It was John the Baptist's preaching of repentance that set the stage for our Lord's ministry. For centuries the voice of

[1] See C. H. Turner, *St. Mark*, p. 11.

prophecy had been silent, when suddenly, in the waste land down near where the Jordan empties itself into the Dead Sea, it rang out, authentic and unmistakable, in John. Later, Jesus was to speak of John as playing the spiritual role of Elijah (9. 13; Matt. 11. 14). Certainly he must have looked like one of the old prophets come alive. Like Elijah (2 Kings 1. 8), he wore a coat of camel's hair and a rough leathern belt about his middle. Like the old prophets, he called to repentance in view of the coming Day of the Lord. (For a fuller account of his preaching, see Matt. 3. 7-12; Luke 3. 7-17.) But there was something new about him — he baptised; hence they called him 'John the Baptiser'. His prophetic preaching soon produced results. There was an exodus from Jerusalem and Judea to Jordan. And John, having preached his message, immersed his penitent hearers in Jordan as a sign of their repentance and a pledge that when the Judgment came, their sins would not stand against them. John did one thing more—he predicted the coming of the Messiah. When he came, John's water baptism would give place to a baptism *with the Holy Ghost*, or, perhaps, as Q puts it, 'with the Holy Spirit *and with fire*'. See Matt. 3. 11; Luke 3. 16.

4. Repentance (*metanoia*)

Not simply 'a change of mind', nor again a being sorry for one's sins, but primarily *a radical return to God* in the prophetic sense: 'O Israel, return unto the Lord thy God.'[1]

6. Locusts and wild honey

Ascetic fare. John's diet was the locust (the insect, not the pod) which the poorer people of the land still eat, and the honey which the wild bees store in the crevices of the rocks.

7. The latchet

The thong fastening the sandal to the foot. The sandals of great persons were commonly tied and untied by slaves.

[1] An educated Jew once said to me: 'In our religion repentance means not "grieve" but "turn", and I think that when our Lord spoke of repentance he meant the same' (W. R. Inge, *Vale*, p. 4).

Note the deep humility of John. (When they compared him with Shakespeare, Sir Walter Scott replied: 'Not fit to tie his brogues.')

So the forerunner played his part; the stage was set for the coming of 'the mightier one'; and when he came, an artisan from Galilee, there was none to acclaim him openly as Messiah.

THE BAPTISM OF JESUS
1. 9-11 (Matt. 3. 13-17; Luke 3. 21-22)

Why did one whom the Christian tradition always regarded as sinless undergo a baptism of repentance for the remission of sins? Not because (as Middleton Murry would have it) he came 'as a sinner among a crowd of sinners' (*The Life of Jesus*, p. 22). Surely the answer is that Jesus discerned the hand of God in John's mission (11. 30), and by his acceptance of John's baptism identified himself with the people he came to save. Right at the outset of his ministry, he was 'numbering himself with the transgressors'. At the end it was to be not otherwise.

At the Baptism, Jesus, we may say, heard the first clear call 'to the dignity and danger of Messiahship'. (Long before this he had known that he was the Son of the Father.) There can be little doubt that the vision and the voice at the Baptism came to Jesus alone, as Mark represents. Further, we must remember that the story is told in symbolical language. The dovelike descent of the Spirit and the voice from the rent heaven are conventional Jewish images to express what is imperceptible to outward eye and ear. But what is their spiritual significance?

The descent of the Spirit upon Jesus means that henceforth he knows himself as 'the anointed of the Spirit' (the very claim he will make in the Nazareth synagogue: 'The Spirit of the Lord is upon me', Luke 4. 18), i.e. divinely empowered for his high task; for, whatever else it means, the Spirit always carries with it the idea of power in which God is active. But observe the precise words of the heavenly voice. God speaks to Jesus through the language of scripture, and most remarkable scripture it is: 'Thou art my Son' is the coronation formula of the Messianic King in Psalm 2. 7. 'The beloved in whom (or rather, with the R.V., 'thee') I am well pleased' is the ordination formula of Isaiah's Servant of the Lord (Isa. 42. 1). This synthesis is no accident. Here is one who knows himself to be at once the Messiah and the lowly Servant of the Lord. And if Jesus knew, even at his Baptism, that as Messiah he must go the way marked out for the Servant of the Lord (Isa. 53 shows the ending of the road), may we not say that, even then, there must have fallen across his path the shadow of a cross?

THE TEMPTATION

1. 12-13 (Cf. Matt. 4. 1-11; Luke 4. 1-13; Q)

After the Baptism there follows, with psychological fitness, the story of the Temptation. For a fuller account of it—an account which must have come from Jesus himself —we are indebted to Matthew and Luke, who derive it from the sayings-source, Q. The whole story, as they tell it, is the highly pictorial record of an intense spiritual struggle—a real, not a sham fight—which Jesus underwent, as, conscious of his Messiahship, he fought his way through a tangle of specious alternatives to a clear vision of the work God had given him to do. But all that Mark records is the fact that he was so tempted in the wilderness.

13. Forty days

An Oriental round number, meaning a considerable time.[1] SATAN. Mark preserves the Aramaic name for the devil. WITH THE WILD BEASTS. To this day there are wild beasts— jackals, wolves, hyenas, foxes, etc.—in the wilderness.

THE PROCLAMATION OF THE REIGN OF GOD

1. 14-15 (Matt. 4. 12-17, Luke 4. 14-15)

A key passage. The Messiah announces that the decisive hour has struck.

[1] Cf. Exod. 34. 28 and 1 Kings 19. 8.

14. Now after that John was put in prison, Jesus came into Galilee

The words seem to hint at an interval between the Temptation and the Galilean Ministry. (Ought we to place in that interval the early Judean Ministry described in John 1-4?) The news of Herod's imprisonment of the Baptist seems to have been the signal for which Jesus was waiting. The fore-runner has run his course; it is now time for the mightier one to appear. The fate of the Baptist Mark will describe later (Mark 6. 14-29). Omit the words 'of the kingdom'. What THE GOSPEL OF GOD IS, the next verse makes clear.

15. If we are to get the background of this verse right, we must turn back to the great prophecies of the Second Isaiah, and particularly such a verse as Isa. 52. 7:

How beautiful upon the mountains are the feet of him that bringeth *good tidings*, that publisheth peace;

That bringeth *good tidings* of good, that publisheth salvation;

That saith unto Zion, *Thy God reigneth*!

There for the first time the word Gospel (good tidings) was used in its theological significance. The messenger is pictured as announcing the return of the exiles from Babylon and the beginning of the real Reign of God—his victory and salvation. Now, says Jesus, that great prophecy, uttered five centuries ago, is coming true! The living God is laying bare his arm; he is about to take to himself his great power and reign! The New Age has begun! Therefore turn again to God and make this Good News of God's Reign your own.

THE TIME IS FULFILLED. The Greek word *kairos* denotes the right, the decisive, the God-appointed time. Paul meant the same thing when he said that it was in 'the fulness of the time' that God sent his Son (Gal. 4. 4).

THE KINGDOM OF GOD IS AT HAND. KINGDOM (*Basileia*) means 'reign' or 'rule'. The Reign of God is to be interpreted, not in terms of nineteenth-century evolution, as a moral disposition in the heart of man, or the gradual amelioration of human affairs, or some far-off terrestrial perfection, but in terms of the Hebrew concept of the living God, transcendent and supernatural, working out his will in history. When Jesus said 'The Reign of God is at hand,' he meant something like this: 'The Eternal is breaking into time for the salvation of men. God is about to visit and redeem his people.' This, then, was the message of Jesus; not as we so often say, 'the Fatherhood of God and the brotherhood of men' (though these may be corollaries of his message), but the proclamation that the New Age was beginning and God breaking decisively into history. REPENT. Again in the prophetic sense, 'Turn to God'. AND BELIEVE IN THE GOSPEL. Accept this Good News as true and make it your own.

In a true sense the rest of the New Testament is commentary on this verse.

THE CALL OF THE FIRST DISCIPLES
1. 16-20 (Matt. 4. 18-22; cf. Luke 5. 1-11)

Jesus has just proclaimed the advent of the Reign of God. His next step is to call four Galilean fishermen to be his disciples. For God's Rule does not operate in a void— it implies a people living under it. It involves the formation of a community. The four men now called are the first recruits for the new community—the new People of God. Others will be called, and then he will choose out twelve to form the nucleus of the new Israel which it is his Messianic mission to create.

The call comes to them in the midst of their daily work, and there is something in the imperious summons which they dare not refuse. To the first pair of brothers Jesus promises that henceforth their task will be to catch not fish but men. Later, Jesus made a parable of the Kingdom out of this saying, the parable of the Drag-net which gathers all sorts of fish (the fish are men) into its meshes. See Matt. 13. 47-50, M.

THE SEA. The Lake of Galilee, a sheet of blue fresh water, some thirteen miles long by six at its widest, lying 682 feet below sea level. Luke, who knew the real sea and its terrors, always correctly calls it 'the lake'.

18. Straightway

One of Mark's favourite words. He uses it some forty-one times and it lends 'an air of breathlessness' to his story. But often it is no more than a connecting link. You may hear Scottish folk often using the word 'syne' in a similar way.

20. Hired servants

Too strong a translation. 'Hands' or 'employees' or perhaps simply 'his men' is all that is implied. Yet the word means that Zebedee was, if not a man of substance, at least not a poor man. Mark wants us to understand that in leaving their father, James and John were not leaving him quite alone.

THE DEMONIAC IN THE SYNAGOGUE

1. 21-28 (Luke 4. 31-37; Matt. omits)

In vv. 21-34 we seem to have the record of one very memorable Sabbath day. The scene now moves to Capernaum on the north-west shore of the lake. It is Sabbath, and Jesus and his disciples 'go to synagogue'. When, as a distinguished teacher, he is invited to address the congregation, everybody is astonished at the clear note of authority in his words. We are not told what the sermon was about; we are told what impression it made. Where their scribes (or professional theologians) were content to retail the *obiter dicta* of noted Rabbis ('Rabbi A says on the authority of Rabbi B', etc.), Jesus speaks as one directly inspired by God. Perhaps Matt. 5. 21-48 will help us to understand the contrast. But the service is suddenly interrupted by a poor demon-possessed man who, with the clairvoyance sometimes found in psychic sensitives of this sort, discerns in Jesus a person of very exalted rank—nay, *the* Person, the Messiah. When Jesus with a word of power exorcises the evil spirit, the miracle but enhances the tremendous impression which his teaching has made, and the news of it spreads like wildfire in the country round Capernaum.

23. A man with an unclean spirit

Jesus' contemporaries attributed many diseases to the influence of malign spirits. Nowadays our diagnosis is rather different—we speak of bacilli, complexes, schizophrenia, etc. Must we reject the Gospel diagnosis (which is often apparently that of Jesus himself)? Let us beware of dogmatism. No one acquainted with the facts will deny that the phenomena ascribed in the Gospels to evil spirits are well attested in both ancient and modern times (though nowadays such phenomena are mostly seen in the mission field among primitive peoples, (See the books of Warneck, Nevius, and Mildred Cable.) Competent observers have declared that these phenomena are only intelligible on the hypothesis of demon-possession. 'I myself,' writes Dr. Walter Lowrie, 'have had experience of driving out evil spirits, which threw young men into convulsions as they went out.'[1]

24. We

The community of evil spirits. THE HOLY ONE OF GOD. A title for the Messiah.

25. Hold thy peace

Literally, 'be muzzled'. COME OUT. No formula of exorcism, no elaborate ritual, no prayer, but only one clear commanding word. What a masterful person Jesus must have been!

26. Torn ('convulsed')

The symptom suggests epilepsy.

27. Follow the R.V. here.

'What is this? A new teaching! With authority he commandeth even the unclean spirits and they obey him.' The word for NEW means 'novel'. They had never heard teaching quite like this before, nor had they seen a man who could so order about evil spirits.

[1] *Jesus according to St. Mark*, p. 74.

PETER'S MOTHER-IN-LAW

1. 29-31 (Matt. 8. 14-15; Luke 4. 38-39)

Fresh from his notable miracle in the synagogue, Jesus
with his four fishermen-disciples enters Peter's home in
Capernaum, to find his mother-in-law 'down' with fever.
Luke, who was a doctor, puts the matter with more precision: 'She was,' he says, 'in the grip of a high fever.' It
may have been malaria, which was common enough in the
damp marshy flats round the lake. Mark tells us that Jesus
took her simply by the hand, though we may guess that he
also spoke some 'therapeutic' word to her. When she is
cured she turns to wait on Jesus and his disciples. So grati-
tude finds practical expression in service.

THE GREAT HEALER

1. 32-34 (Matt. 8. 16-17; Luke 4. 40-41)

This story serves to remind us that the healing miracles
recorded in the Gospels are only a selection of typical cases
from many that have not been recorded. The point of the
apparently pleonastic AT EVEN WHEN THE SUN DID SET is that
the Sabbath day was now technically over, and scrupulous
Jews might bring out their sick without fear of breaking the
Law. When Mark tells us that ALL THE CITY WAS GATHERED
TOGETHER AT THE DOOR, we need not take him literally.
That is the hyperbole common in the Oriental, but (let us
add) not unknown in the Occidental world. Observe that
Jesus did not allow the demoniacs to speak. Premature asser-
tions of his Messiahship might ruin his whole mission.

RETIREMENT

1. 35-39 (Luke 4. 42-44)

After the ardours of the previous day, Jesus slips away
before dawn into a solitary place, feeling the need of communion with his Father. For even the Son of God must
refresh himself by prayer amid the hurly-burly of his minis-

try. When his presence is missed, impulsive Peter and some others (Peter must have told this story) 'track him down'. They feel that Jesus is missing a great chance: they must fetch him back. Jesus replies that not Capernaum alone, but all 'the country towns' must hear the Good News of the Kingdom. And he goes forth to preach and heal in the synagogues of all Galilee.

35. And there prayed

'No Christology is true which makes a Christ for whom prayer is either unnatural or impossible.'[1]

38. The next towns

Literally, 'village-cities' (kōmopoleis). Towns as to size, villages as without walls. FOR THEREFORE CAME I FORTH. From Capernaum, not from God; though that was true, too.

THE CURE OF A LEPER
1. 40-45 (Matt. 8. 1-4; Luke 5. 12-16)

The experts seem agreed that what the Bible calls 'leprosy' (in Lev. 13-14, here and elsewhere) was some skin disease (or diseases) less severe than what we know as leprosy. Yet this 'leper', if he obeyed the instructions of the Law, must have been a pathetic sight—his clothes rent, his hair loose, his upper lip covered, and his hoarse cry 'Unclean, unclean' —as he came running to Jesus. Instead of standing afar off, as a leper should, he knelt down before Jesus: 'If thou wilt, thou canst make me clean!' He did not doubt Jesus' power; he doubted his good will. Compassion (or, some MSS. say, 'anger'; see the notes) welled up in Jesus' heart and he touched him: 'I do will. Be cleansed.' He was healed at once. Then, 'assuming a severe aspect', Jesus commanded silence about the cure, bidding the man go at once to the priest in Jerusalem and do everything that a cured leper should do. But the man disobeyed Jesus' command about silence; he shouted his cure on all hands, so that the posi-

[1] H. R. Mackintosh (quoted by Dorothy Wilson in *The Teachers' Commentary* on this passage).

tions of healer and healed were reversed, and, while the leper moved freely now in the towns, Jesus had to remain outside them if curiosity were not to be aroused.

41. Moved with compassion

Some MSS. read 'moved with anger'. If this be the true reading (as many believe), we can only guess at the cause of Jesus' anger. Was it because the leper, admitting his power, doubted his good will? Or was it indignation at the evil in the world that can reduce a man to such a hideous plight?

43. Straitly charged him

The Greek word (*embrimēsamenos*) means literally 'snorting', and is used to describe strong feeling. We may picture our Lord assuming a severe aspect and speaking intensely.

44. For the Levitical regulations about 'leprosy', its diagnosis and the procedure following cure, see Lev. 13-14. FOR A TESTIMONY UNTO THEM. For a proof to all and sundry of the reality of the cure.

II

In 2. 1-3. 6 we have a series of incidents—often called 'the Conflict Stories'—in which we trace the ever-growing conflict between Jesus and the synagogue authorities, a conflict which eventually compels Jesus to withdraw to the lakeside.

THE PARALYTIC

II. 1-12

(MATT. 9. 1-8; LUKE 5. 17-26)

A very graphic story. The scene is probably Peter's house in Capernaum. The news of Jesus' return has brought a dense crowd to the front door of the house, where Jesus PREACHED THE WORD UNTO THEM (literally, 'was telling them the message', i.e. the Good News of the Reign of God). There comes a sudden interruption: four men carrying a paralysed man try to force a way through the concourse. Failing, they climb the external stairway to the roof of the house, dig a hole through the layer of beams, brushwood, and mud (sending, no doubt, an unpleasant shower on those below), and lower the invalid on his mattress to the feet of Jesus. This is the very importunity of faith which Jesus was later to praise in parable (see Luke 11. 5-8 and 18. 1-8). 'My child,' says Jesus, looking affectionately into the sufferer's face, 'your sins are forgiven.' The faces of some scribes in the crowd grow dark. This is sheer blasphemy. Only God can forgive sins. Yet here is a man invading the prerogative of God, and the earth has not swallowed him up! Jesus reads their thoughts. 'Which is easier,' he asks, 'to tell this paralytic that his sins are forgiven, or to bid him pick up his mattress and walk?'

Neither was easier. To say these words as Christ meant them was as hard as to cure the paralytic. Two deeds are set in contrast, both impossible to man and alike easy to God. Then, in order to show his power to the scribes, Jesus says: 'Arise and walk'; and in effect bids them infer that the hidden work of forgiveness has as surely followed his first words as the obvious cure had followed his second command. He did the miracle which they could see that they might know that he had done the other one which they could not see. Thus there are two miracles here—the physical one and the spiritual. For it is important to note that Jesus claims the power not only to announce the forgiveness of sins, but, as God's representative, actually to forgive them; in short, to come forward as the divine Pardon incarnate. And both the act of forgiving and the cure of the paralysis are equally works in demonstration of the Kingdom. It was the latter claim—to be the divine Pardon incarnate—which the scribes pronounced blasphemy. Men to-day find themselves in the same position. They are faced with a dilemma. Either Jesus is a blasphemer and the sense of sins forgiven which many win at his hands is a pernicious illusion, *or* Jesus has power, in the name of God, to release men from their sin. We must decide one way or the other.

1. In the house

Better, with R.V. margin, 'at home'. Peter's home, the only home Jesus had after he left Nazareth.

4. For the press

For the crowd. THE BED (*krabbatos*) a colloquial word meaning 'mattress' or 'shake-down'; a rug which could be spread on the floor at night and rolled up in the daytime.

5. When Jesus saw their faith

'Faith is a thing that can be seen. You can see it in a man's face, you can see it in a man's actions. These friends of the

sick man evidently had faith of a sort, and a great deal of it.
To this faith Jesus responded with his whole heart. Here
it would seem as if a man might be saved by other people's
faith. That does not seem incredible to me, for I have been
saved (perhaps) by my mother's faith, and I reflect that few
would be saved if vicarious faith were not effectual for salvation.'[1]

8. Perceived in his spirit
Read their thoughts.

10. The Son of Man
The first occurrence of our Lord's favourite name for himself. Derived from Dan. 7. 13, it is a veiled name for the
Messiah. See the essay on *The Son of Man* at the end of this
chapter.

12. We never saw it on this fashion
Mark means us to understand that the people felt they were
in the presence of something uncanny—a *mysterium tremen-
dum et fascinans*—what Otto calls 'the numinous'.

THE CALL OF LEVI
2. 13-17 (Matt. 9. 9-13; Luke 5. 27-32)

Levi we naturally identify, on the basis of Matt. 9. 9, with
Matthew, supposing Levi to be his original and Matthew
(which means 'gift of God') his apostolic name. He was a
publican or taxgatherer in Herod's employment, with his
place of business at the toll-house on the great road that
ran from Damascus through Capernaum to the sea. There,
in that 'house of extortion', Jesus found a 'vessel of elec-
tion'. Ruskin has pictured the call in his vivid English:

This man, busy in the place of business, engaged in the
interests of foreign governments—thinking no more of an
Israelite Messiah but only of Egyptian finance and the
like—suddenly the Messiah passing by says 'Follow me'
and he rises up, gives him his hand, 'Yea, to the death!'

[1] W. Lowrie, *Jesus according to St. Mark*, p. 98.

and absconds from his desk in that electric manner on the instant, leaving his cash-box unlocked and his books for whoso list to balance! A very remarkable kind of person, it seems to me.[1]

Later, there is a banquet, whether in Jesus' house[2] or Matthew's is not clear. If, as scholars generally hold, the house was Matthew's, it is clear that Jesus acted as the host. At the banquet there was a nondescript gathering of 'tax-gatherers and sinners'. The former were doubtless Matthew's old colleagues, a class of men much execrated by good Jews not merely because they served Herod, the puppet of Rome, but because extortion was a basic principle of their trade. The term SINNERS probably means 'irreligious persons', all who did not come up to the Pharisees' standard of Law observance. The sight of Jesus playing the host to these renegades and reprobates was too much for the scribes, who were the experts on the interpretation of the Law. 'Why,' they said to Jesus' disciples, 'does your master hold table-fellowship with the riff-raff?' Jesus makes a pointed reply:

> Those who are well do not need the physician, but those who are sick. I did not come to invite righteous people, but sinners.

If we ask, 'Invite to what?' the answer is, 'To the banquet of the Kingdom of God' (cf. the parable of the Great Feast, Luke 14. 16-24, Q). Of course, there is a dash of irony in Jesus' use of the word 'righteous'. It does not mean that Jesus has no call for good people. It means that the Gospel is not for the 'unco guid'—people like the Pharisee in the parable (Luke 18. 9-14) who are sure of their own righteousness and know not that all our righteousnesses are 'as filthy rags' in the sight of God. It would be true to say that this word of Jesus strikes the keynote of the Gospel. The new thing in Christianity is not the doctrine that God saves sinners. No Jew would have denied that. It is the assertion 'that God loves and saves them *as sinners* without waiting for them to become righteous and deserving of salvation'.

[1] Ruskin, *St. Mark's Rest*, para. 174.
[2] See note on 2. 1.

St. Paul echoed his Lord when he wrote: 'God proves his
love to us in that while we were yet sinners Christ died for
us' (Rom. 5. 8). And this is the authentic and glorious doctrine of true Christianity in any age.

15. For there were many

Probably disciples. A hint that the number of Jesus' followers was rapidly growing.

16. The scribes and Pharisees

Read with the R.V. 'the scribes of the Pharisees'. Most of
the scribes or professional teachers of the Law were Pharisees.

17. To repentance

These words, obviously imported from Luke 5. 32, should
be omitted.

THE QUESTION OF FASTING
2. 18-22 (Matt. 9. 14-17; Luke 5. 33-39)

Fasting on particular days of the week, though not enjoined by the Law, was the sign of piety *par excellence*, and
the disciples of both the Pharisees and the Baptist practised
it. If Jesus and his friends had any ambition to appear as
really religious men, they ought to have followed suit. But
they did not. To the question, 'Why not?' Jesus replied that
fasting would be as incongruous in that glad time (he meant
the Messianic age now dawning) as it would be at a marriage
feast. (Observe that the Talmud refers to certain privileges
granted to the bridegroom and his friends, e.g. permission
to omit the *Shema*, or Creed, which every pious Jew recited
morning and evening.) He went on to speak darkly of the
removal of the Bridegroom (as John 3. 29 shows, a veiled
reference to his Messiahship): clear proof that, in the full
tide of the Galilean ministry, Jesus knew that as Messiah
he would have to die.
    To this he added two little parables: the Patched Garment
and the Wineskins. (Jesus often used a pair of parables to

make the same point.) If we translate them into modern English, they become much clearer:

> No one sews a patch of unshrunk cloth on an old coat. If he does, the patch pulls away from it—the new from the old—and a worse tear is the result. No one pours freshly fermented wine into old wineskins. If he does, the wine will burst the wineskins and the wine be lost.

The point of both is the folly of trying to accommodate the new to the old—the Kingdom of God to the outworn forms of Judaism. You cannot combine Law and Grace. It was precisely this that the Judaisers tried to do in Galatia. Paul, like Jesus, knew that it could not be done.

19. With our Lord's saying about the joy of the Kingdom, compare Rom. 14. 17: 'The Kingdom of God is . . . joy in the Holy Spirit.'

22. Bottles

Better, 'wineskins'. These were made from goatskins. The animal was skinned from the neck by cutting off the head and the legs and then drawing the skin back. After being steeped in tannin and filled with a decoction of bark for a few weeks, the skins were sewn up at the neck and the seams pitched.

LORD OF THE SABBATH
2. 23-28 (Matt. 12. 1-8; Luke 6. 1-5)

This incident belongs to the Galilean harvest time, i.e. May. The Law (Deut. 23. 25) allowed a hungry man to pluck ears of corn in passing through a neighbour's field, but forbade reaping on the Sabbath day; and to pluck ears of corn and rub them in the hands (cf. Luke 6. 1) was a kind of reaping.

Jesus' reply to the Pharisees' attack on his disciples is to appeal to the action of David when he and his friends ate the holy bread which had lain for the previous week in the sanctuary at Nob (see 1 Sam. 21. 1-6). But why does Jesus single out David? Is it merely an appeal to a notable precedent, as though to say, 'Our great ancestor did this, and do you blame my disciples for this trifling act?' Or is it because the Messiah (as all admitted) is a son of David, and David a type of the Messiah?

Jesus proceeds:

The Sabbath was made for man, and not man for the Sabbath. So that the Son of Man is Lord even of the Sabbath.

What is the true interpretation of this utterance? Is it just that the Sabbath exists for man's good and not vice versa? That is to say, it is a specific instance of the general truth that man is greater than any institution. This is the usual view of scholars. But may not the point be in the final part of the saying? Let us recall that the Sabbath enjoined in the Law was regarded as a sort of ritual foretaste of the true Sabbath, i.e. the Messianic Age. (It is so interpreted in Heb. 3 and 4). The Law Sabbath was the shadow; the Messianic Age, when it came, was to be the reality—a time of pure peace and joy. If this is the right clue, the reason why his enemies were so angry at Jesus' attitude to the Sabbath (he seemed to go out of his way to heal on it) is that his actions and attitude involved the claim to be the Messiah, and therefore Lord of the Sabbath. 'Jesus was acting as Lord of the Sabbath, interpreting the Sabbath as a ritual anticipation of the Messianic Age. When he heals on the Sabbath, it is because the Messianic Age has arrived' (A. G. Hebert, *The Throne of David*, p. 12; see ch. 6 for a very interesting discussion of this whole problem).

26. Abiathar

A slip of memory. In the O.T. story the high priest is not Abiathar, but Ahimelech (his father).

ESSAY I—THE SON OF MAN

Our Lord's favourite name for himself was the Son of man. In the Synoptic Gospels it occurs some seventy times, and always on his own lips. Some of the examples are of a quite general kind, as 'The Son of man came eating and drinking' (Luke 7. 34); but, for the most part, Jesus' uses of the title group themselves round two main motifs: (*a*) humiliation, as, 'The Son of man must suffer many things' (Mark 8. 31); and (*b*) exaltation, as, 'Ye shall see the Son of man sitting at the right hand of power and coming with the clouds of heaven' (Mark 14. 62). Whence did Jesus derive the title, and in what sense did he use it?

The Source of the Phrase

In the Old Testament 'son of man' sometimes means simply 'man' (e.g. Ps. 8. 4). But modern scholars are now more or less agreed that Jesus' use of the title is to be traced to Dan. 7. That chapter describes the seer's vision of the four beasts, then it proceeds (v. 13): 'I saw in the night visions, and, behold, there came with the clouds of heaven *one like unto a son of man*, and he came even to the Ancient of days (i.e. the eternal God), and they brought him near before him. And there was given him dominion, and glory, and a kingdom,' etc. Later follows the interpretation of the seer's vision: the four beasts signify four kings, the heads of four world-empires. The 'one like unto a son of man' represents 'the saints of the Most High' (i.e. the People of God).

Now it seems clear that Jesus regarded himself as that 'Someone' who was destined to receive from God glory and a kingdom. That 'Someone' was the Messiah, i.e. himself. But if so, another interesting corollary follows. In Dan. 7. the 'one like unto a Son of man' represents the People of God. He is 'a societary person'. Jesus must therefore have regarded himself as the representative or head of the People of God. His task, then, as the Bearer of God's Rule to men, was to create this People of God. And, for him, beyond any doubt, the twelve disciples (significant number) were its nucleus.

Jesus' use of the Phrase

Of the fourteen uses of the title in Mark, twelve fall after Peter's confession at Caesarea Philippi. Some scholars have

therefore concluded that Jesus used the title only after that
event, and explained the two earlier uses (Mark 2. 10, 28)
in the sense of 'man'. This is a very precarious inference.
Why should Jesus not have used the title before Peter's
confession? To be sure, he avoided the title 'Messiah'; but
for that there were good reasons. There is no good reason
why he should not have chosen from the beginning another
title to express his unique relation to the Kingdom of God.
That title lay to hand in 'the Son of man'. It was not a
common title for the Messiah, and, in virtue of its mysterious
nature, Jesus could use it even before Peter's confession
without the disciples finally concluding that he was the
Messiah.

Now the dominant idea in the title is that of *sovereignty*.
Thus in Dan. 7. the 'one like unto a Son of man' receives
a kingdom from God. He is the destined Bearer of God's
Reign to men. It is in accordance with this that Jesus often
associates the title with the thought of his ultimate triumph
and exaltation (see Mark 8. 38 and 14. 62). No matter what
present appearances may be, as the Son of man he is destined to triumph and receive dominion.

But (and this is the new, original, and startling thing) with
the idea of sovereignty Jesus combined the idea of *suffering*.
'The Son of man must suffer many things'; 'The Son of
man came not to be served but to serve and to give his life
a ransom for the many' (Mark 8. 31 and 10. 45). The references to suffering for 'the many' take us back to Isaiah's
great picture of the Suffering Servant of the Lord (Isa. 53).
In short, Jesus knew himself called to fuse in his own person
and destiny the two roles of the Danielic Son of man and
the Isaianic 'Servant of the Lord'. 'He was born to suffer,
born a king.'

III

THE MAN WITH THE WITHERED HAND

III. 1-6

(MATT. 12. 9-14; LUKE 6. 6-11)

THIS, the last of the 'Conflict Stories', is another Sabbath incident. Jesus had so often healed on the Sabbath (our Gospels, which are only a selection, contain no less than seven healing miracles on the Sabbath) that his enemies came to the synagogue on this Sabbath to watch him rather than to worship God. The Rabbis laid it down that only if life were in danger was healing on the Sabbath permitted. Sitting there in the synagogue was a man with a withered hand. What would Jesus do? Jesus' reply is to bid the man step into the middle. Then he rounds on his critics, 'Which is the better way of observing the Sabbath—by having the desire to heal, as I have to this man, or by having the desire to kill, as you have towards me?' Then, with a look in which anger mingled with grief, he bade the man stretch out his hand. The healing of the man was the signal for the Pharisees to troop out of the synagogue and make common cause with the Herodians against Jesus. They had seen once again the claim to be 'Lord of the Sabbath'. Now it was *guerre à outrance*.

There is a striking parallel to this cure in the *Journal* of John Banks (1637-1710). His hand and arm became para-

lysed, and the doctors were helpless. In a dream-vision he
was bidden go to George Fox at Swarthmore and get him
to touch his shoulder. Fox did so with the words: 'The Lord
strengthen thee both within and without.' That evening, at
supper, Banks found he could use his hand again. Later he
told Fox of the cure. 'John, thou mended, thou mended,'
said Fox. 'Yea, very well,' said Banks, 'in a little time.'
'Well,' replied Fox, 'give God the glory.'[1]

1. A withered hand
Hand-paralysis followed by contracture. Luke says that it
was his right hand which was affected, and an old tradition
makes the man a bricklayer.

5. When he had looked round about on them with anger
Jesus was not always 'meek and mild'; in the presence of
evil he could blaze out in indignation, and surely such
'anger' is a necessary element in the highest character.
HARDNESS. Callousness, or perhaps moral blindness (Armi-
tage Robinson).

6. The Herodians
Cf. Mark 12. 13. A group of men who in these troubled
times pinned their hopes on the Herodian dynasty.

RETIREMENT TO THE LAKE
3. 7-12 (Matt. 12. 15 ff.; Luke 6. 17-19)

The rising hostility of the scribes and Pharisees now compels Jesus to quit the synagogues and (like Wyclif and Wes-
ley) to preach in the open air by the lakeside. But official
ostracism cannot stop popular enthusiasm, and a great
crowd from all parts of Palestine follow him to his new
sphere of work. A small boat is requisitioned to prevent
Jesus being mobbed by the multitude. And with his preaching Jesus continues his work of healing. Once again we learn
that certain demoniacs, with a kind of spiritual clairvoyance,
declare Jesus to be the Messiah (literally, 'Son of God'),

[1] See E. R. Micklem, *Miracles and the New Psychology*, p. 97

and once again they are silenced. 'This was not the time, neither were these the heralds.'[1] A premature disclosure of his Messiahship might ruin everything.

THE CHOICE OF THE TWELVE

3. 13-19 (Matt. 10. 1-4; Luke 6. 12-16)

An important stage in the Gospel history. Out of the growing number of his followers, Jesus marks out twelve men to be disciples in the fullest sense of the word. The number is the number of the tribes of Israel. The Messiah has begun to create the New Israel. The Twelve are to be the nucleus of the new People of God. The scene of this epoch in ecclesiastical history (for such in very truth it is) is 'the hill-country' or high land near Capernaum. In calling his twelve men, Jesus had a twofold purpose: (1). 'that they might be with him', go to school with him, learn of him, and (2). 'that he might send them forth to preach', etc., i.e. he was preparing them for the time when they should go forth as his 'apostles' or 'messengers'.

The list of the Twelve which follows is one of four lists in the New Testament. The others are to be found in Matt. 10. 2-4; Luke 6. 14-16; and Acts 1. 13. For eleven out of twelve names the lists tally:

> Peter and Andrew
> James and John
> Philip and Bartholomew
> Thomas and Matthew
> James the son of Alphaeus and Thaddeus (or Judas, son of James)
> Simon the Zealot and Judas Iscariot

For 'Thaddeus' (Matthew and Mark) Luke gives us 'Judas, the son of James'; but these may well be different forms of the same name (Thaddeus—Theudas—Judas). Moreover, since John couples Nathanael with Philip, just as the Synoptists couple Bartholomew (son of Tolmai) with

[1] Bengel, *Gnomon*, on this passage.

Philip, we may guess that Nathanael and Bartholomew were one and the same person.

PETER is, of course, the Greek equivalent of the Aramaic CEPHAS, and means 'rock-man', a surname given him by Jesus, perhaps to suggest his rugged aspect and character. BOANERGES, the surname which Jesus gave the sons of Zebedee, is perhaps a hint that there was something of the thunderstorm in their temper (cf. Luke 9. 51-56; Mark 9. 38, 10. 37). Matthew, as we have already seen, is probably Levi. The second James is called 'son of Alphaeus', no doubt to distinguish him from the son of Zebedee. But SIMON THE CANAANITE (A.V.) is certainly wrong. Canaanite should be 'Cananaean', an Aramaic word which Luke rightly renders 'Zealot'. This Simon evidently belonged to that group of extreme Pharisees called the Zealots, the 'nationalists at all costs' who were determined to drive out the Roman oppressor at the point of the sword. The last in the list is the traitor Judas, whose second name probably means 'man of Kerioth', a village in Judea (Josh. 15. 25). He was the only non-Galilean in the band.

Twelve men, then, belonging to what we would call the lower middle class—a taxgatherer, an extreme nationalist, four fishermen, and the rest we know not what—such were the men Jesus chose to be the nucleus of the new People of God.

14. Whom also he named apostles

These words, which have been imported by a scribe from Luke 6. 13, should be omitted.

THE BEELZEBUL CONTROVERSY

3. 20-30 (Matt. 12. 22-32; Luke 11. 14-23)

(*Note.*—The sayings-source Q also contained an account of this controversy. See Luke 11. 14-23 and cf. Matt. 12. 22-30, where Matthew blends the Markan and Q accounts.)

Mark begins by telling us of the anxiety of Jesus' kith and kin about him, goes on to describe the charge of 'black magic' which some Jerusalem scribes brought against him,

and after relating the controversy, records Christ's words
about his 'real brethren'.

The scene cannot be far from Nazareth, for his family are
well aware of the enthusiasm his mission is evoking. Some
have already begun to dismiss Jesus as a madman, and
Jesus' relatives, hearing the common talk, go in search of
him. Meanwhile some scribes, perhaps at the invitation of
the local Pharisees, have come down from Jerusalem on a
commission of investigation. Unable to deny his power to
heal the demoniacs, they attribute it to collusion with the
arch-fiend. Jesus' reply is an appeal to common sense:
'How can Satan cast out Satan?' (As we might say: 'Dog
does not eat dog, does he?'). Then he develops his reply in
two little parables: the divided kingdom (24-26) and the
strong man bound (27). The point of the first is obvious.
'Satan is not a fool. He has his kingdom; and like all king-
doms, its strength lies in its unity. Why should Satan raise
civil war in his own realm?'[1] In the second, the stronger
man is Jesus himself, who, so far from being in league with
Satan, has overmastered him (a reference to the Temptation)
and is taking possession of his goods—human souls in thrall
to Satan (a reference to his exorcisms). Jesus ends his reply
with a stern saying. Men can be forgiven all sorts of sins
and slanders save one—the sin against the Holy Spirit.

21. For they said

People said, like the French *on disait*.

22. He hath Beelzebub

He is possessed by Beelzebul. This seems to be the correct
form of the name. Beelzebul, or Baalzebul, was an inten-
tional caricature of Baalzebub. Baalzebub means 'Fly-god'.
The Jews said, Baalzebul, i.e. 'Filth-god', and applied it to
Satan.[2]

---

[1] T. W. Manson, *The Mission and Message of Jesus*, p. 377.

[2] The alternative explanation is 'Lord of the House'. In that case
there may be a play on words in Jesus' reference to stronger man
mastering the strong man (=the devil) in his house, i.e. the world.
Jesus is the true, Beelzebul the false 'Lord of the House'.

28 f. Verily I say unto you

A favourite phrase of Jesus. It is always a signal that something specially important or solemn is to follow. IS IN
DANGER OF ETERNAL DAMNATION. Follow the R.V. 'is guilty
of an eternal sin'. 'Forgiven sins,' says Morison, 'are sins
that are taken up by God from the burdened conscience and,
as it were, cast behind his back . . . but unforgiven sins
abide for ever on the souls that committed them.'[1]

It has been said that these words about 'the unpardonable
sin' have caused more pain and misunderstanding than any
others in scripture. What is the sin which cannot be forgiven? The context makes it clear that the unforgivable sin
is to ascribe to the devil works which are manifestly of God.
The sin of the scribes was that, face to face with works of
mercy and love, with what they knew to be good, they
nevertheless deliberately declared them to be things of the
devil. With this saying compare also John's word about
'the sin unto death' (1 John 5. 16). It has been said with
reason that what Christ has in mind is not so much an
isolated act of sin as a condition of soul; a condition of soul
so diseased that it cannot be forgiven, not because God is
not ready to forgive, but because the man does not want
forgiveness. In this saying 'Christ warned the Pharisees, as
he warns us, that a man may so take evil to be his portion,
may so hug it to himself that at last—at last—repentance is
impossible'.[2] For such a state of soul, even Christ and his
atonement provide no remedy. Many people (one thinks of
Bunyan and Cowper in particular) have been haunted and
tormented by the belief that they have committed the unpardonable sin. To all such we may say (in the words of
Ryle): 'There is such a thing as sin which is never forgiven,
but those who are most troubled about it are most unlikely
ever to have committed it.'[3]

[1] Quoted in *Commentary on St. Mark* (T. M. Lindsay).
[2] G. Jackson, *A Young Man's Religion*, p. 249.
[3] Quoted in *Commentary on St. Mark* (T. M. Lindsay).

CHRIST'S REAL BRETHREN

3. 31-35 (Matt. 12. 46-50; Luke 8. 19-21)

Resumption of the story of Jesus' family. His BROTHERS are not (1) his cousins (Jerome's view), or (2) his half-brothers (the Epiphanian view), but (3) his real brothers, the younger sons of Mary. There is no evidence that Mary strongly disapproved of her Son's mission. Rather, hearing the common talk, she came, with a mother's anxiety, to take him home. Further, our Lord's reply conveys no censure— 'he despises not his mother, but places before her his Father'[1]—but instruction. There is, he says, a deeper relationship than the merely natural one: true kinship with him is spiritual. 'Founder's kin' are all who hear God's word and do it. Cf. Luke 11. 27 f. and John 15. 14.

[1] Bengel, *Gnomon*, on this passage.

IV

PARABLES OF THE KINGDOM
IV. 1-9
(a) THE SOWER
(MATT. 13. 1-9; LUKE 8. 4-8)

MARK now records some of the parables in which Jesus spoke to the people about the Reign of God. Before we consider them it will be well to say something about parables. There are five main points to remember.

1. Jesus did not invent the parable. There are parables in the Old Testament—witness Jotham's Parable of the Bramble (Judg. 9. 7-15) and Nathan's Parable of the Ewe Lamb (2 Sam. 12. 1-7)—and the Rabbis also used them. But it was Jesus who brought the art of the parable to perfection:

> In his hand
> The Thing became a trumpet, whence he blew
> Soul-animating strains—alas, too few!

2. A parable, as the etymology shows, is a comparison—a 'like-saying'. (How often Jesus says, 'The Kingdom of God is like . . .') In its simplest form it is a figurative saying, whether metaphor or simile (e.g. 'A city set on a hill cannot be hid'). When this is expanded into a picture (e.g. the Patched Garment) or a story (e.g. the Sower), we get what is usually called a parable.

3. A parable is not an allegory. In an allegory (e.g. Paul's

allegory of the Olive Tree (Rom. 11. 16 ff.) or Bunyan's
Pilgrim's Progress) each detail is meaningful and indispens-
able to the understanding of the whole. In a parable, as a
rule, there is one main point, and the details serve to enforce
and embellish that one point. In studying any parable, therefore, we must always ask, What is the central point for the
sake of which Jesus told this parable? *N.B.*—But Jesus did
occasionally use allegory, e.g. the allegory of the Wicked
Husbandmen (Mark 12. 1-12).

4. Jesus' purpose in using parables was (*a*) to convey
truth in a pictorial form, since 'truth embodied in a tale'
is always much more memorable (we might forget a sermon
on forgiveness, but who that heard it could forget the Parable of the Prodigal Son?); and (*b*) to stimulate his hearers
into thought and action. The parable invites the hearers to
form a moral judgment on the character or the actions of
the people in the parable, and then to apply that judgment
to their own lives and situation.

5. Jesus' parables were all related, in the first instance, to
the historical situation created by Jesus' ministry. For
example, the Parable of the Prodigal Son was told as a reply
to certain critics who had complained that he consorted too
freely with publicans and sinners. Thus the parables of the
Kingdom let us into the secret of what the coming of Jesus
and the Kingdom meant to his contemporaries. By the same
token they interpret to us our own experience. For, as Pro-
fessor Dodd says, 'The historical crisis of the gospels is re-
enacted in the crises that come upon men and nations. God
in his kingdom, power and glory, confronts us with judgment and mercy, with challenge and opportunity. In such
situations the parables spring out of their historical setting
and "speak to our condition".'[1]

Mark begins by painting the scene by the lakeside. So
great is the crowd eager to hear Jesus that he has to choose
a floating pulpit. Sitting there in the stern of a fishing boat,
he faces the multitude for whom the sloping beach forms a
natural theatre. Then, perhaps pointing to a man actually
sowing in sight of the people, he tells them the Parable of

[1] From article on 'Parables' in *In His Steps*

the Sower. At first sight it looks to be simply the story of
a farmer and his fortunes, but as the closing words warn us,
it is a great deal more.

What, then, is the central point of this Parable of the
Kingdom? In the parable we hear Jesus thinking aloud about
the fortunes of his work in Galilee, with its mixture of
failure and success, and the point surely is this: the seed
(which is the Good News of the Reign of God preached by
Jesus) is all good, but for its development everything depends on the ground in which it falls. So we may say that
the parable illustrates the different receptions given to the
appeal of Jesus and the Kingdom of God, and is meant to
impress a sense of responsibility upon his hearers. It says
pictorially: 'Take heed how ye hear.' So understood, it
might be better called 'The Parable of the Four Different
Soils'.

5. Stony ground
Rock with a thin dusting of soil on the top.

9. He that hath ears, etc.
A *nota bene* to the parable, meaning: this is more than a
pleasant story.

THE PURPOSE OF PARABLES
4. 10-12 (Matt. 13. 10-15; Luke 8. 9-10)

In private Jesus explains the reason for parables. But his
words, as they stand in the A.V., read as if he used parables
deliberately to blind and befog the common people. This is
absurd. The explanation probably is that an Aramaic word
de has been rendered into Greek by *hina*, i.e. 'that' (in order
that) when it should have been rendered by *hoi*, i.e. 'who'
(but see T. W. Manson, *The Teaching of Jesus*, p. 78). We
may then paraphrase Jesus' words as follows: 'To you, my
disciples, is revealed the secret (literally, mystery) of God's
Reign, but the parabolic method must be used with the
multitude who, as Isaiah also found, are lacking in spiritual
insight.'

10. They that were about him, with the twelve

A retinue of followers plus the chosen twelve. These are contrasted with 'the outsiders'.

12. A free version of Isa. 6. 9 f.

THE INTERPRETATION OF THE SOWER
4. 13-20 (Matt. 13. 18-23; Luke 8. 11-15)

Because the interpretation allegorises the parable, many modern scholars think that, as it stands, it is the work of the early Church. This may be true, though it is not certain. But since (a) the interpretation draws out what we take to be the meaning of the parable as Jesus told it, and since (b) it seems based on genuine reflections of Jesus about the causes which led men to reject his message (persecution, distracting anxiety, the love of money), we may fairly claim that it is true to 'the mind of Christ'. As we have it, it is a moving sermon on 'How to hear the Gospel', and it faces each one of us with the searching question: 'Which soil do I represent? The hard soil? Or the shallow soil? Or the crowded soil? Or, by God's grace, the good soil?'

17. Offended

Made to stumble. A technical term for backsliding.

19. The cares

Worries, the thorns of the spiritual world.

20. Some thirtyfold, etc.

These percentages mean that there are different degrees of responsiveness to the Gospel. The old classification was 30 per cent—the mass of Christians; 60 per cent—Gospel celibates; 100 per cent—the martyrs.

THE HIDDEN AND THE REVEALED: MEASURE FOR MEASURE
4. 21-25 (cf. Luke 8. 16-18)

A little collection of sayings, most of which have their parallels in Q. Their general purport is that secrets are given to the disciples in trust for the world, and a man's advance in knowledge of the Kingdom is in proportion to his loyalty to what has previously been entrusted to him.

21. For 'candle' and 'candlestick' read 'lamp' and 'stand'. The BUSHEL (*modios*) is a vessel holding about two gallons (dry measure). Translate: 'meal tub'. The meaning of this little parable of the lamp and the meal tub is that the light of God's revelation is not to be hidden away (as the Jewish leaders were hiding it; see Matt. 23. 13; Luke 11. 52), but to serve as a beacon to light all men to the truth (cf. Matt. 5. 15; Luke 11. 33 and Luke 8. 16).

22. This difficult saying must refer to the future manifestation of the Kingdom of God. Though now, in a sense, a secret, it will not always be so (Mark 9. 1). Cf. Matt. 10. 26; Luke 12. 2 (Q).

24. 'Take heed what you hear. The measure you give will be the measure you get, and still more will be given you.' The disciples' attentiveness to the teaching will be the measure of the profit they get from it. Cf. Matt. 7. 2 and Luke 6. 38.

25. One of our Lord's paradoxical sayings. A man's spiritual resources increase or dwindle according to the use he makes of them. 'If we do not use, we lose.' It is the Parable of the Talents (Matt. 25. 14-30) in a nutshell. Cf. Luke 19. 26 and Matt. 25. 29.

(b) THE SEED GROWING SECRETLY

4. 26-29 (Mark only)

This parable, peculiar to Mark, is one of the most cryptic of all the parables. At first sight it seems as if the Kingdom were being compared to the *process* of silent and secret growth. If this is so, Jesus is saying in effect, 'God's Reign is a secret divine force working itself out in the world, whether men will or not'. But it is more likely that the emphasis falls not on the growth, but on the *harvest*. There are two clues to what is probably the true interpretation.

In the first place, note that the last verse of the parable echoes Joel 3. 13. Speaking of the Day of the Lord and the time of world judgment, Joel cries: 'Put ye in the sickle, for the harvest is ripe.' Second, our Lord likened the advent of God's Reign in his own mission and ministry to the coming of harvest time. Thus, in the charge to the Twelve, he says: 'The harvest truly is plenteous, but the labourers are few. Pray ye therefore the Lord of the harvest that he send forth labourers into his harvest' (Matt. 9. 37 f.; Luke 10. 2). Likewise, in the Fourth Gospel, he says: 'Say not ye, There are yet four months and then cometh the harvest? Behold, I say unto you, Lift up your eyes and look on the fields, that they are white already unto harvest' (John 4. 35).

This is a parable of 'realised eschatology'. We should call it the Parable of the Reaper rather than of the Seed Growing Secretly. It says: 'The long period of growth—blade, ear, and full corn in the ear—is over and the harvest-tide is here. The seed of God's purpose sown long ago in Israel and ripened through the generations is now a crop waiting to be reaped. Let us to the gathering of souls for God.'

29. When the fruit is brought forth

Rather, 'when the fruit yields', i.e. 'when the grain is ripe'.

(c) THE MUSTARD SEED

4. 30-32 (cf. Matt. 13. 31 f.; Luke 13. 18 f.)

This, the third parable from agriculture, also stood in Q, where it probably formed a pair with the Parable of the Leaven.

The most natural interpretation is 'Small beginnings, great endings'. The Reign of God now being manifested in Jesus' mission and message may seem a fact of little importance; yet it is really the beginning of a new era and is destined to become the greatest thing on earth, and to include Gentiles as well as Jews in its embrace.

31. A grain of mustard seed

A proverbial Jewish expression for a very small thing.

32. Greater than all herbs

The mustard seed in Palestine sometimes grows into a herb
standing eight feet high. SO THAT THE FOWLS OF THE AIR
MAY LODGE UNDER THE SHADOW OF IT. The 'birds of the air'
was a common rabbinical phrase for the Gentile nations.
Jesus clearly envisages Gentiles in the Kingdom. Cf. Luke
13. 29. But we may go further. The image of the bush or
tree, so great that the birds roost in its shadow, is taken
from Dan. 4. 12, 21, where the kingdom of Nebuchadnezzar is likened to such a tree. Daniel interprets the tree
to signify the greatness of Nebuchadnezzar's dominion,
which is to reach to the ends of the earth. Even so, in this
parable, Jesus predicts that the Reign of God, now present
in germ in his mission, will one day overspread the world.
Is not that prophecy coming to pass to-day in the fact of
the World Church?

CONCLUDING REMARKS ON THE PARABLES
4. 33-34 (Matt. 13. 34-35)

What we have in this chapter (Mark says) is only a selection. Jesus used the parabolic method because it suited well
the spiritual capacities of his hearers. When he had the
disciples alone, he expounded everything fully to them,
'giving preference over the multitudes to those who were
eagerly desirous of his wisdom' (Origen).

THE STILLING OF THE STORM
4. 35-41 (Matt. 8. 23-27; Luke 8. 22-25)

The scene now shifts to 'the other side', i.e. the east side
of the lake. After the labours of the day the disciples take
Jesus aboard their boat and seek to put six miles of water
between him and the crowds. But the lake is subject to
sudden storms which sweep down the funnel-like valleys
dividing the surrounding highlands. The boat, caught in a
fierce squall, begins to fill, and even the hardy fishermen
begin to fear for their lives. So they rouse Jesus, who is fast

asleep in the stern: 'Do you not care if we perish?' Jesus
awakes, addresses a word of power to wind and wave, and
the storm subsides. The disciples are filled with awe.

What shall we think of this story? Some of us make
valiant efforts to rationalise it. We say that what Jesus stilled
was the storm of fear in the disciples' hearts, or we put it
all down to 'coincidence': the storm did subside after Jesus
spoke to it, and the disciples argued '*Post hoc, ergo propter
hoc*'. Either way, we abandon Mark's record. Let us
examine our doubts. Why do some of us who accept Christ's
healing miracles boggle at a nature miracle like this? One
reason, no doubt, is that, while we can believe that Jesus
influenced men's bodies through their minds, we can see no
mental bridge between Jesus and the storm. Another is that
we tacitly accept 'the steel-and-concrete' conception of the
universe as a fixed and closed system (though that so-called
scientific dogma is fast dissolving in our time). Before, however, we reject this nature miracle, let me suggest three con-
siderations which seem to me to weigh down the scales in
the direction of acceptance. First, when we Christians pray
God, as we do, to deliver 'those in peril on the sea', are we
not in fact praying for a nature miracle to happen? Second,
if we grant, as most Christians do, that God raised Jesus
from the tomb—and a dead body is as much a part of the
material order as the winds and waves of Galilee—why
should we reluct at the idea that Christ, with God's help,
was able to control the elements? Third, and most important, if we accept, as most Christians do, the truth of the
Incarnation (i.e. if we believe that the divine Spirit was
uniquely incarnate in Jesus Christ), we have no right to lay
down the limits of what Jesus could or could not do. Pro-
fessor T. E. Jessop has summed up the point very neatly:
'If the universe is dominated by a Spirit, miracles are possible; if by a Spirit that is love, probable; and if the Spirit
has become incarnate, this miracle would make further ones
very probable indeed.'[1]

37. For 'full' read 'filling'.

[1] *The Christian Faith*, p. 15.

38. A pillow

The leathern cushion for the steersman. MASTER translates the Greek *didaskalos*, which in turn represents the Hebrew 'Rabbi'. That was the disciples' title for Jesus before the Resurrection. After he had risen, it was always 'Lord', a title of religious reverence. Why, then, do so many Protestants prefer to call Jesus 'Master'? Do we, or do we not, mean to call him only 'Teacher'?

39. Be still

Literally, 'be muzzled', 'be gagged', as though he were speaking to the demon of the storm.

40. Why are ye so fearful? How is it that you have no faith?

The cure for fear, says Jesus, is faith. He says: 'Can you not yet learn to leave everything to the care of the great Father, as I do? And is not he upon the water as well as upon the land?'[1] 'Jesus proposes to cast out all petty and ignoble fears by one great and noble fear—fear of God. And the fear of God which Jesus inculcated was not terror, but trust. There is nothing but the fear of God can make us truly courageous.'[2]

41. And they feared exceedingly

This time they were afraid of Jesus—and were not rebuked. But their fear was a religious feeling: it was the sense of awe in the presence of something and someone uncanny. Again and again the disciples had this fear. The last word of this Gospel—'for they were afraid'—expresses the same feeling. One wonders if the modern Church has not so domesticated Jesus as to kill all healthy and wholesome 'fear' of him.

[1] 'The boat which carried the hope of the world could not sink. (W. Temple, *Nature, Man and God*, p. 268, n. 2).
[2] Lowrie, *op. cit.*, p. 208 ff.

V

THE GERASENE MANIAC

V. 1-20

(MATT. 8. 28-34; LUKE 8. 26-39)

A GRIMLY graphic story to illustrate our Lord's mastery over the powers of evil. The scene is the east side of the lake, but precisely where? Were the people of the district 'Gadarenes', 'Gerasenes' or 'Gergesenes' (all three names being found in the MSS.)? Was the place Gadara, Gerasa or Gergesa? Neither Gadara (six miles south of the lake) nor Gerasa (in Gilead, twenty miles east of Jordan) is geographically possible. But a place now called Khersa, which has a cliff, ruins, and old tombs, and is near the lake, will suit, and we may assume that this is the place.

Observe, first, certain difficulties in the story: (a) the name Legion (though we need not take it literally to mean 5,000!); (b) Jesus' command to proclaim the cure; and (c) the strange fate of the swine. Can we explain these?

The main facts are clear enough. Here was a 'possessed' person of a very unusual kind—an extreme case, we should probably say, of 'delusional insanity'. There was a remarkable cure at Christ's word. A sudden access of terror seized a nearby herd of swine and caused them to run over the cliffs into the lake, where they were drowned.

Now observe that the background of the story is *Gentile*, not Jewish. For (1) the district is Decapolis, and (2) a herd of swine on purely Jewish soil is improbable (cf. Lev. 11.

7 f.). Once we realise that the background is Gentile, the
difficulty about Christ's command to proclaim the cure dis-
appears. On Gentile soil, such a proclamation would not be
fraught with danger.

The capital difficulty is the destruction of the swine. Must
we believe that Jesus deliberately willed it? It is, I think, a
true instinct which makes us shrink from attributing such
a malignant prank to one whose love for beast, bird, and
flower is writ so large in the Gospels. Since this is a popularly
told story, some rationalisation is surely permissible. We
need not doubt that Jesus cured this extraordinary case of
delusional insanity; but we may well doubt whether he
caused the deliberate destruction of so many innocent swine.
Rather, we may surmise, the maniac's wild frenzy while he
was being cured set the nearby swine into a stampede and
led to their being drowned.

The sequel to the cure is interesting. The people of the
neighbourhood come out to see for themselves and find the
ex-maniac CLOTHED (had one of the Twelve a spare tunic?)
and ' in his sober senses'. But the loss of their precious pigs
meant more to them than the cure of their fellow country-
man, and they were soon clamouring for the departure of
Jesus. (We may guess that they missed a good deal by their
clamour, for it is hard to suppose that Jairus alone in the
Palestine of that day had a sick daughter in need of healing.)
The ex-maniac, for his part, desired to join the disciple
band. Jesus refused his request: he had a mission for him—
to return to the home he had exchanged for the tombs and
to be a witness for God and his Christ in that dark land of
the Decapolis.

5. In the mountains and in the tombs crying

Cf. the experience of the traveller Warburton (*The Crescent
and the Crown*, ii, 352): 'On descending from the heights of
Lebanon I found myself in a cemetery. The silence of the
night was now broken by fierce yells and howlings, which
I discovered proceeded from a naked maniac, who was
fighting with some wild dogs for a bone.'

7. Son of the Most High God

There is evidence that 'the most high God' was used as a title for God on both Jewish (cf. Gen. 14. 18) and Gentile soil.

19. The Lord (*Hŏ Kurios*)

Here means God, not Christ (cf. Luke 8. 39).

20. Decapolis

A league of ten Greek cities stretching from Damascus to the Arabian Desert and including Gadara, Pella, Gerasa, and Damascus.

THE DAUGHTER OF JAIRUS AND THE WOMAN WITH THE ISSUE OF BLOOD
5. 21-43 (Matt. 9. 18-26; Luke 8. 40-56)

Now follows one of Mark's vividest narratives. On his return to the west shore of the lake, Jesus is confronted by a large crowd, when suddenly out of it comes one of the synagogue notables called Jairus (or Jair) with an urgent request: 'My little daughter is dying. Do please come and lay your hands on her that she may recover and live.' This is the importunity of faith, and Jesus goes off with Jair, while the crowd follows at his heels.

But Jair is not the only person with faith. In the crowd there is a woman 'whose misery is as old as Jair's daughter'. For twelve years she has suffered from a hæmorrhage which has made her ceremonially unclean and a social outcast. All her means have been spent on doctors' fees—without avail. Now quietly, nervously, she pushes through the crowd in the rear of Jesus, in hope to steal a miracle, saying to herself the while, 'If I but touch his garment, I shall be cured.' Her faith is at once rewarded, and she knows from her bodily sensations that her misery is over. Jesus feels that touch, feels the power flow out from him, and his searching glance wanders over the crowd till it lights on 'the faithful thief'. Tremblingly she tells him the whole truth. 'Daughter,' he says, 'your faith has made you well. Go in peace, and may your trouble never worry you any more.'

Before he has stopped speaking there comes a message for Jair: 'Don't worry the Rabbi. Your little girl is dead.' Most would have turned back at the message. Jesus (as D. S. Cairns put it)[1] 'risked his whole reputation in going on'. 'Fear not,' he replies to Jair, ignoring the message, 'only go on believing.' Taking Peter, James, and John, he enters the stricken house to find a scene of loud lamentation. At once he ejects the lugubrious sympathisers. Then, with the tender words that her mother no doubt used every day to wake her, he takes her by the hand and sets her on her feet. And, while amazement fills the room, he 'reminds a too happy father that his little girl would be the better of food'.[2]

22. One of the rulers of the synagogue
Each synagogue had its college of elders who supervised the synagogue worship. The nearest modern equivalent is a Presbyterian Kirk Session.

26. Had suffered many things of many physicians
Dr. Luke, understandably enough, tones down this phrase in his narrative.

27. Touched his garment
The garment was probably the *tallith* or prayer shawl. Matthew and Luke say that she touched the hem, i.e. the fringe or 'ribbon of blue' commanded by Moses in Num. 15. 37-39.

28. For she said (*elegen*)
Kept saying over to herself, 'If I but', etc.

33. Fear and trembling
Why? Because she, an unclean woman, had touched a holy Rabbi and made him unclean, too.

34. Daughter
The only time Jesus so addresses a woman. Tradition names her Veronica, and declares that it was she who gave Jesus

[1] *The Faith that Rebels*, p. 220.
[2] T. R. Glover, *The Conflict of Religions in the Early Roman Empire*, p. 125.

the handkerchief to wipe his face on the way to Calvary, so that afterwards it was impressed with a portrait of his face.

36. Heard
The Greek participle (*parakousas*) means either 'ignoring' or 'overhearing' (R.V. margin).

37. Peter, James, and John
The inner circle in the Twelve, 'elect of the elect', who were later to be alone with him on the Mount of Transfiguration and in the Garden of Gethsemane.

38. The loud lamentation would come mostly from the professional mourners—a common feature in the East. These Jesus excluded, for only the real mourners were to be comforted; only they needed it.

39. The damsel is not dead, but sleepeth
Our Lord's words, if taken literally, mean that the girl was in a state of suspended animation.[1] On the other hand, Matthew and Luke thought that she was actually dead. If so, this narrative, with those of the Widow of Nain's Son and the Raising of Lazarus, is evidence that Jesus was able not only to heal the sick, but to recall people from the state of death. In that case it may be that Jesus wished to put a meaning on her death more worthy of those who believe in a God who is not baffled by bodily death. As he said later: 'He is not the God of the dead, but of the living.'

41. Talitha cumi
Mark preserves for us the actual Aramaic words which Jesus used. But the A.V.'s 'Damsel, I say unto thee, arise', is far too stiff. In Scots it would be: 'My wee lass, get up.'

43. Again the injunction to silence. Notice also the humanity of our Lord. How easily he turns from supernatural to natural: 'She will need something to eat.' Even the child's mother, it has been said, was not so motherly as Jesus.

---

[1] In favour of this view note that the verb is *katheudo*, which denotes natural sleep, not *koimaomai*, which is often used of the sleep of death. Cf. our 'cemetery'.

VI

THE REJECTION AT NAZARETH
VI. 1-6

(MATT. 13. 53-58; LUKE puts this visit to Nazareth earlier. See Luke 4. 16-30)

Jesus now leaves Capernaum to preach in the villages of Galilee and begins twenty-five miles away in his 'native country' of Nazareth. At first his teaching in the synagogue 'astounds' them, but they cannot forget that the Rabbi, whose fame is throughout all Galilee, had once been their village joiner. 'There is always a shadow under the lamp,' says the Indian proverb. The Nazarenes were too near to appreciate the splendour of his words and works, and their unbelief left Jesus marvelling.

2. What wisdom is this?

There was an undeniable depth and wisdom in his words which puzzled them, because everybody knew that he had been an artisan without (as we would say) a university education. In the Fourth Gospel the Jews say: 'How is it that this man has learning when he has never studied?' (John 7. 15). MIGHTY WORKS, literally 'powers' (dynameis). The two common words for 'miracle' in the Gospels are dynamis and semeion. The first emphasises that the miracle is a manifestation of the great power of God; the second, which is commonly used in the Fourth Gospel, means a 'wonder with a meaning in it'.

3. The carpenter

Like the smithy in more recent days, the carpenter's shop was a centre of village life, and in it were made practically all the agricultural implements—ploughs, harrows, yokes, etc. THE SON OF MARY. Presumably she was now a widow. THE BROTHER OF JAMES AND JOSES, AND OF JUDA AND OF SIMON. A pious family, for these four bore the names of patriarchs, Jacob, Joseph, Judah, and Simeon. (And the eldest, Jesus or Joshua, was called after a great deliverer.) Of the four brothers, the only one we know much about is James. Disbelieving in Jesus in the days of his flesh, he came to belief through an appearance of the risen Lord (1 Cor. 15. 7) and rose to be head of the Mother Church in Jerusalem.

4. Probably a current proverb, like our 'familiarity breeds contempt'. In the *Logia* of Jesus, discovered in Oxyrhynchus at the beginning of this century, the saying runs: 'No prophet is acceptable in his own country, *neither does a physician work cures on those who know him.*'

5. He could do there no mighty works (Matt. 13. 58 says: 'He *did* not there . . .)

A moral, not a physical inability. The miracles of Jesus were not magic, they needed faith. 'Unbelief and contempt of Christ,' says wise old Matthew Henry, 'stop the current of his favours.' Even so, in our day, when we (so often) reduce Jesus to our own proportions, he can do no mighty works because of our unbelief. Is not this one primary cause of the Christian failure in our day? HE MARVELLED. Once he marvelled at the great faith of a Gentile centurion (Luke 7. 9); here he marvels at the great unfaith of his fellow countrymen.

THE MISSION OF THE TWELVE

6. 7-13 (Matt. 10. 1-15; Luke 9. 1-6)

N.B.—The mission is 'one of the best-attested facts in the life of Jesus', since it is attested in all four sources—Mark, Q, L., and M. On the connection between the Mission of the Twelve and the Mission of Seventy (recorded only by Luke), see *The Mission and Message of Jesus* by Major, Manson, and Wright, pp. 365 f.

First the call, then the choice, and finally the commission of the disciples. The time has come to test the results of their training (and to prepare them for future missions beyond the Cross). Jesus sends them forth two by two, no doubt on the scriptural and common-sense basis that 'two are better than one' (Eccles. 4. 9). If we ask what is the purpose of the Mission, the answer is that it was to gather the People of God. (See my book, *The Unity of the New Testament*, pp. 57-8.) He sends them out 'like men carrying the Fiery Cross through a Highland glen', and before they go he gives them their 'marching orders'.

First, they are to travel light. Dispensing with food, collecting-bag or money, they are to carry only a stick (the traveller's *vade mecum*), a pair of sandals, and one tunic. (Matthew denies them even sandals and stick, and Luke the stick. Mark must be right here.)

Second, they are to preach and heal. Mark tells us simply that they preached 'repentance'. But from Luke and Matthew we learn that they were to preach the advent of God's Reign: 'Heal the sick and say, The Reign of God has come nigh upon you' (Luke 10. 9; cf. Matt. 10. 7). This was the self-same message as Christ's (Mark 1. 15). They were to be messengers of the Kingdom; their credentials the power to exorcise and heal.

Third, they are to observe certain rules of hospitality. With well-wishers they are to stay; but, if others reject their message, they are to waste no time, but quit them with a solemn gesture.

Fourth (and this point we derive not from Mark, but from Q), they are to remember whose ambassadors they are. 'He who receives you receives me, and he who receives me, receives him that sent me' (Matt. 10. 40; Luke 10. 16; cf. Mark 9. 37). They are the accredited envoys of Jesus, and, through him, of the King of kings.

Then the curtain falls on their mission, and we hear no

more of the 'apostles' or 'messengers' until they return and report to Jesus.

8. Scrip

'Wallet' (R.V.). The Greek word (*pera*) means either (1) a travelling bag, or (perhaps likelier) (2) a beggar's collecting-bag. Wandering Cynic preachers—the mendicant friars of antiquity—often carried such bags.

10. There abide

'If ye have judged me to be faithful to the Lord,' said Lydia to Paul at Philippi, 'come ye into my house and *abide there*' (Acts 16. 15).

11. Shake off the dust under your feet for a testimony against them

Oman has called this symbolic gesture 'the sacrament of failure'. Its meaning is: 'We have nothing in common with you—not even the dust of the road.' At Pisidian Antioch, Paul and Barnabas used this symbol (Acts 13. 51).

The remaining words of the verse 'Verily . . . city', not in the R.V., have been imported from Matt. 10. 15 and should be omitted here.

THE MURDER OF THE BAPTIST

6. 14-29 (Matt. 14. 1-12; Luke 9. 7-9)

Mark has already mentioned John's imprisonment (1. 14). Now, perhaps to fill up the time-interval until the return of the Twelve from their mission,[1] he related the Baptist's fate.

Jesus' fame had now reached the ears of Herod Antipas, the ruler of Galilee and Perea and a son of the notorious Herod the Great. Popular speculation about Jesus was taking various forms. Some thought he was John the Baptist risen from the dead; others identified him with Elijah, who, according to Mal. 4. 5, was to come back to herald

[1] Or was John's death a signal to Jesus? At his baptism by John Jesus heard his call to be Messiah. John's imprisonment was a signal to stand forth in his place. Was John's death now a signal that, the Forerunner having suffered martyrdom, the Messiah must prepare for the Cross?

Messiah's advent; and others thought he must be one of
the old prophets, perhaps Jeremiah (Matt. 16. 14). Herod
himself preferred the first conjecture.

Then Mark tells how the Baptiser met his end. At first,
when John had outspokenly condemned Herod's adulterous
marriage with Herodias, his brother Philip's wife, Herod
had contented himself with imprisoning John in the lonely
fortress of Machaerus down near the Dead Sea (we owe this
last detail to Josephus, the Jewish historian). Though Herod
stood in awe of John as a holy man, Herodias 'had it in
for him' (as the Greek of v. 19 has it). Her opportunity
came when a party of Herod's chief civil officials and high-
ranking officers were celebrating his birthday, probably at
Machaerus. The daughter of Herodias, whose name we
learn from Josephus was Salome, so charmed the men by
her dancing that Herod, possibly in his cups, swore to grant
her any favour she craved. Salome consulted her mother,
who at once saw her chance of being rid of John. Herod
dared not now break faith with Salome, so a guard was
despatched to execute John.

14. King Herod

His real title was tetrarch, i.e. ruler over a fourth part of
his father's dominions. HE SAID. The true text is probably
'they [i.e. people] said'. John in life had done no miracles
(John 10. 41), but John risen from the dead might be expected to have strange powers.

17. His brother Philip's wife

Not Philip the tetrarch of the north-east regions (Luke 3. 1),
who ultimately married Salome, but another. HE DID MANY
THINGS. The better reading is *polla eporei*—'he was much
perplexed'. The whole sentence means: 'When he listened
to him he was greatly exercised, and yet he liked to listen to
him.'

21. His lords, high captains, and chief estates of Galilee

In modern terms, 'his chief officials and generals and the
notables of Galilee'.

25. In a charger

On a large flat dish, as though it were one of the courses at the banquet; a grisly witticism.

26. Reject her

Break faith with her.

THE FEEDING OF THE FIVE THOUSAND

6. 30-44 (Matt. 14. 13-21; Luke 9. 10-17; cf. John 6. 1-14)

The twelve 'missionaries' now returned and reported to Jesus, who, perhaps noting the tell-tale signs of fatigue, suggested a time of retreat. If they had stayed where they were quietness would have been impossible, for there was a two-way traffic of 'comers' and 'goers', and sometimes it was hard to snatch even a meal. So the boat was launched, and they set off for an unfrequented spot near the lakeside. But many recognised them as they tried to slip away and, trekking along the shore, were waiting for Jesus and his disciples when the boat touched land.

So, moved with pity—for in that solitary place the crowd seemed like so many shepherdless sheep—Jesus taught them until the evening shadows began to fall. Then he fed them.

The Feeding of the Five Thousand, as Mark records it, leaves us asking questions. Where did the feeding take place? Can we credit the creative miracle which Mark indubitably means to relate? Was the feeding only a miracle, a *dynamis* or 'power', or was it something more? We cannot conclusively answer all these questions; but with the hints supplied elsewhere by Mark, with our general conception of our Lord's ministry, and with some help from John's narrative, we can make better sense of the whole happening than was possible to some of the older interpreters.

To take the question of the miraculous first. Many attempts have been made to 'rationalise' the miracle. Thus it has been suggested that Jesus and his disciples set the example of sharing their provisions and that the multitude followed suit. Or it has been said that the whole narrative is history, except the statement that they were all 'filled' (Schweitzer). But all such explanations do violence to the evidence as Mark gives it, and in the last resort it seems best to take the miracle 'on faith'.

'Every evangelist supposed our Lord to have wrought a creative act; and for myself, I have no doubt that this is what occurred. This, however, is credible only if St. John is right in his doctrine of our Lord's person. If the Lord was indeed God incarnate, the story presents no insuperable difficulties'.[1]

But was the feeding only a work of creative power, a *dynamis*? Or was it also a *semeion*, a wonder with a meaning in it? Even Mark (6. 52 and 8. 17-21) hints that there was in it a mystery not fully understood, and when we examine St. John's account we note that Jesus follows up the miracle with a discourse on the Bread of Life. There is here a valuable clue. Let us recall, first, that Jesus, like the Old Testament prophets, made free use of symbolic action. Let us also recall that he once told a parable of the Kingdom in which he likened it to a Great Supper or Feast—a feast to which guests were invited with the words 'Come, for all things are now ready' (Luke 14. 16-24; Matt. 22. 1-10). We may, then, say that when Jesus 'made the men all sit down' and gave them food at the hands of his disciples, he was acting out his own parable—he was signifying by word and act that the new life of the Kingdom was now available for men. The bread was the Bread of the Kingdom, or, in John's idiom, 'the Bread of Life'. So the Feeding of the Five Thousand might well be named 'The Galilean Lord's Supper'. It was the precursor of another meal, the Last Supper, when Jesus consecrated twelve men to the life of the Kingdom of God. Did Jesus mean this Galilean Supper to be a moving sacrament of farewell for the multitude and a pledge and foretaste of the celestial banquet in God's eternal Kingdom?

30. Apostles

The word here means simply 'missionaries'; it has not yet acquired its more specialised sense.

[1] W. Temple, *Readings in St. John's Gospel*, p. 75.

31. Come ye yourselves apart into a desert place

The Christian worker may surely here find Dominical warrant for a time of respite from his labours.

34. When he came out

Out of the boat.

37. Two hundred pennyworth of bread

PENNY is the Greek *denarius*, a labouring man's daily wage in those days (Matt. 20. 2). 'Shilling' would be a less inadequate translation.

38. Five, and two fishes

John tells us that they were barley loaves, and that it was Andrew who found 'the lad' who carried them in his bag (6. 8 f.).

39. The green grass

It was 'the sweet o' the year'—springtime. A year must have gone by since Jesus' disciples plucked the ears of corn. John tells us that it was near Passover time (6. 4).

40. In ranks (*prasiai*)

Literally, 'garden-beds'. A vivid word which implies either the rectangular orderliness of the marshalled crowd or the picturesque multi-coloured appearance which it presented.

41. He looked up to heaven, and blessed

Jesus, like the house-father at a Jewish meal, said the grace. So also he did at the Last Supper; and it is interesting to find that bread and fish appear on early Christian frescoes as a symbol of the Eucharist.[1] This, incidentally, confirms the interpretation we have put upon the story of the Feeding of the Five Thousand.

43. Twelve baskets full of the fragments

The Greek word (*kophinos*) denotes the wicker basket in which each Jew carried his day's food.

[1] 'In the catacombs of Rome the sacrament of the Eucharist was commonly represented not by a picture of thirteen in an Upper Room, but by a company reclining on the ground with seven baskets and two fish conspicuously in evidence' (Lowrie, *Jesus according to St. Mark* p. 275).

THE WALKING ON THE WATER

6. 45-52 (Matt. 14. 22-33; cf. John 6. 15-21)

Why did Jesus *constrain* the disciples to embark after the feeding? Here, as so often, John's Gospel supplies the clue. 'Jesus therefore, perceiving that they were about to come and take him by force, to make him king, withdrew again into the mountain himself alone' (6. 15). After 'the Galilean Lord's Supper' there was something of a crisis; if he had not acted with promptitude the crowd would have swept him away and acclaimed him as the King Messiah of their dreaming. So Jesus, after practically forcing the disciples to embark, persuaded the crowd to depart, and himself withdrew to the 'hills' to discover in solitary communion what was his Father's will for him.

When the disciples were 'well out to sea' the wind rose and soon they were 'straining' at the oars for dear life. It was about 3 a.m., when suddenly, by the light of the Paschal moon, they were aware of Jesus walking on the water. At first they thought they had seen a ghost, but through the storm came the familiar voice of their Master: 'Be of good cheer: it is I. Be not afraid.' They took him aboard, and suddenly the wind lulled.

It is of no use to pretend that we know *how* it happened. What we do know is *what* happened, the triumphant love and power that came to them in the hour of their desperate need. Once again we get an idea of the tremendous impression that Jesus made upon those who knew him. And yet, as Mark says, the disciples did not yet understand all that they might because they were still all too spiritually slow in mind.

45. Bethsaida

The geography here is not clear, perhaps because Mark was a native of Jerusalem and did not know Galilee intimately. Mark says the boat was making for Bethsaida (i.e. Bethsaida Julias at the north-east end of the lake where the Jordan enters it), whereas John says that the disciples' destination was Capernaum. Eventually they landed at Gennesaret.

48. The Romans divided the night into four watches. The fourth watch would be between three and six o'clock in the morning.

49. It had been a spirit

Perhaps, being superstitious like most sailors, they imagined they had seen the malevolent spirit which had raised the storm.

52. They considered not

They did not understand about the loaves. 'They ought to have inferred from the bread to the sea. The more exercised faith is, the more it becomes accustomed to discern the marvellous works of God.'[1] HARDENED. Blinded or dulled.

HEALING AT GENNESARET

6. 53-56 (Matt. 14. 34-36)

The boat touched land not at Bethsaida on the north-east corner of the lake, but at Gennesaret, a charming little vale, three miles long by one broad, south of Capernaum. Perhaps the change of destination was due to the contrary wind which had blown them out of their course. They were no sooner disembarked than people recognised them, and began to bring their sick on pallet beds to the Great Healer in village, town, and farm. Even to touch his garment was enough to effect a cure, and many were so healed.

[1] Bengel, *op. cit.*, on this passage.

VII

CONCERNING CLEANLINESS, Etc.

VII. 1-23

(MATT. 15. 1-20)

T HE Pharisees from Jerusalem, with some of their theologians, the scribes, now take an increasing interest in Jesus and his disciples. Observing that some of Jesus' disciples are not careful to wash their hands before meals—the issue is not hygienic, but religious—they raise the whole question of religious purity. The question is whether religious impurity can be contracted *from the outside*. The scribes said it could. Jesus said it could not.

The core, then, of this section is in the Pharisees' question (vv. 1, 2, and 5) and in Jesus' answer (v. 15). But Jesus uses the occasion to raise other points at issue. It will therefore conduce to clarity if we divide it up into three parts:

(a) The Dispute about Defilement (1-8)

Some of Jesus' disciples did not trouble to wash their hands before meals. This was abhorrent to the Pharisees, not so much because they were zealots for cleanliness, but because such hands were *ceremonially* unclean and rendered any food unclean which they ate. At this point Mark remembers that he is writing for Gentiles who could not be expected to know about ceremonial uncleanness; so he inserts a parenthetical explanation. 'The Pharisees,' he explains, ' never take a meal without scrupulously washing their hands.

They wash similarly when they come in "from market" for their midday meal, besides observing a good many other rules about washing drinking cups, etc. In all this they are following the tradition of the Elders.' (This tradition, or oral law, tried to solve all questions on which the written law had nothing specific to say.)

The Pharisees therefore want to know why Jesus' disciples are deliberately flouting what we might call 'Catholic custom'. Jesus' first riposte is a telling quotation from Isa. 29. 13. 'Isaiah,' he says, 'depicted hypocrites like you to the life when he said:

> 'This people honours me with their lips, but their heart is far from me: in vain do they worship me, teaching as doctrines the precepts of men.

'Lip-service, not heart-worship, is what you give God, while you exalt man-made rules and regulations into divine commands.' As an illustration of what he means, Jesus cites

(b) The Case of Corban (9-13)

Let us begin by paraphrasing the passage. Jesus says, in effect: 'The fifth Commandment, given by God through Moses, plainly bids a son (or daughter) honour his parents, and death is the penalty prescribed for him who reviles them (Ex. 20. 12; 21. 17). But you scribes, by your legal fiction of Corban, permit a man to evade the positive command of God. This is what I mean when I say that you stultify God's law by your man-made tradition. And I could quote a good many other examples like it.'

What was CORBAN? The word (which is Hebrew) means 'dedicated' or 'given to God', and was a formula used in vows. If an angry or unscrupulous Jewish son wished, he might, with the sanction of the religious authorities, utter the formula 'Corban'—i.e. formally dedicate to God (or the Temple use) his earnings which would otherwise have gone to the support of his parents. The whole thing was a legal fiction, for the goods thus dedicated did not need in fact to go 'for religious purposes'. Apparently some scribes in Jesus' day emphasised so strongly the sanctity of such a vow that they insisted on its being kept, even if it conflicted with a man's plain duty to his parents. 'This mere travesty of a vow,' says Jesus, 'you scribes allow to override the positive command of God.' It annuls God's law instead of safeguarding it. (The case Jesus takes need not have been hypothetical. There may have been a *cause célèbre* which was being discussed in the bazaars of Galilee at that time.)

(c) The Truth about Purity (14–23)

Jesus now turns from the scribes to tell the people wherein true religious purity consists. Not from without inwards, but from within outwards, he says, is the true order in this matter of cleanness. And inward defilement—the defilement of the heart by the sins of the heart—is the only possible defilement in God's sight. The only cure is to purify the heart. As Montefiore puts it: 'Things cannot be religiously clean or unclean: only *persons*. And persons cannot be defiled by things: they can only be defiled by themselves, by acting irreligiously. This principle destroys with a prophet's blow the terrible incubus from which all ancient religions suffered, that certain objects or religious states are in themselves taboo or religiously unclean. The world is profoundly indebted to Jesus for this liberating and clarifying word.'

Afterwards, in private, the disciples desire Jesus to amplify his *parable*, i.e. short, pithy saying (v. 15). Jesus tells them that it is out of the heart that all evil purposes proceed. Twelve such are named. All these are the evil fruits of an evil heart. These, and these only, make a man unclean.

3. Oft

The better reading in the Greek means 'with the fist', i.e. up to the wrist—the prescribed ritual hand-washing for pollution in the market-place. THE TRADITION OF THE ELDERS. The complicated rules about ritual purity which Jewish theologians had deduced from Leviticus in order to make the Law applicable to every phase of life.

4. Which they have received to hold

Which they traditionally observe. Omit 'and of tables'; probably no part of the true text.

8. Omit also, with the R.V., 'as the washing of pots . . . ye do'.

9. Means: 'You have a fine way of rejecting the commandment of God in order to maintain your tradition.'

11. In the A.V. is not clear. Translate rather: 'But you say, "If a man tells his father or his mother, What you would have gained from me is CORBAN" (that is, given to God), you no longer allow him to do anything for his father or mother.'

19. Purging all meats

Grammatically, this goes with 'he saith' of v. 18: 'This he said . . . purging (i.e. pronouncing clean) all meats.' Mark means that our Lord's dictum made an end of the Mosaic distinction between clean and unclean meats. Was this Peter's comment as he told the story? Cf. Acts 10. 15: 'What God hath cleansed, that call not thou common.'

22. An evil eye

Envy or malevolence. BLASPHEMY. Rather, 'slander'. FOOL-ISHNESS. Moral wrongheadedness or senselessness: the quality which makes all the rest incurable. What a catalogue it is! 'Jesus knew what was in man', no psychoanalyst better. Then what, asks Lowrie, becomes of our optimistic Jesus who was so convinced of man's essential goodness that we sometimes wonder why he judged it necessary to die for him?[1]

WITHDRAWAL TO TYRIAN TERRITORY: THE FOREIGN WOMAN'S DAUGHTER

7. 24-30 (Matt. 15. 21-28)

N.B.—Matthew alters Mark's narrative considerably and adds to it.

The Galilean ministry is over. Jesus now retires into Tyrian territory, wishing perhaps to avoid the hostility of Herod Antipas; wishing also to train the Twelve for the

[1] Lowrie, *op. cit.*, p. 299.

Cross and all that lies beyond it. But, even on Gentile soil, he cannot wholly escape notice, and soon he is discovered by a Gentile woman, who begs him to heal her demon-possessed daughter. For a moment, half whimsically and with a smile, Jesus tests the woman. 'Salvation,' he says in effect, 'belongs first to the Jews. Is it right to take the food meant primarily for the children (the Jews) and give it to the dogs (the Gentiles)?' (The sense is: 'I am a Jew. You know how Jews regard people like you. "Children" and "dogs" is the conventional way of putting it. What have you to say if I put it that way?') The woman rises splendidly to the occasion. 'True, sir,' she answers, 'the children have the first right to the food, but even the little dogs below the table come in for a share of the children's scraps.' This brilliant reply, combining at once a ready wit and a persistent faith, delights Jesus. He grants her request, and the woman, returning home, finds her daughter lying exhausted on the bed, but on the way to recovery.

This cure, like that of the centurion's servant, was wrought at a distance. We cannot rationalise it. To faith it is credible, and its secret must be sought (1) in the realm of prayer, and (2) in the person of Jesus. Jesus, being who he is —one in perfect communion with the source of all healing— is able, by prayer, to release that healing for the benefit of whomsoever he will.

In such a story as this we have a foreshadowing of the Gospel for the wider world. It is, in Bacon's phrase, 'a promise of the children's bread to Gentiles'.

24. Into the borders of Tyre and Sidon

Omit, with R.V. margin, the words 'and Sidon'.

26. A Greek, etc.

GREEK here means 'Gentile'. The woman was PHOENICIAN born, SYRIAN by political division. There were other Phoenicians—Liby-Phoenicians—dwelling in the North African region of Libya.

27. The dogs

A common Jewish term for Gentiles. Jesus takes the harsh edge off the word by using the diminutive (*kunaria*): 'little dogs', 'puppies'.

28. Yes, Lord (*Nai, Kurie*)

Better 'Yes, sir.' '*Yes, Lord.* Was not that a masterstroke? She snares Christ in his own words' (Luther).

30. She found the devil gone out

Note that the paralytic broke through outward obstacles, blind Bartimaeus through hindrances raised by his fellow men, but this woman through an apparent hindrance from Christ himself (Trench). The first act of salvation in the Gentile world, it has been said, was an answer to persistent prayer.

THE CURE OF THE DEAF STAMMERER

7. 31-37 (found in Mark only)

Our Lord now leaves Tyrian territory and takes a circuitous route to the lake via the territory of the Decapolis. The motive of this roundabout journey was probably a desire to give a wide berth to Herod. Mark relates the journey in one sentence, but it must have taken many weeks, even months.

Somewhere on the journey there is brought to him a deaf man with a bad impediment in his speech. The account of his cure is rather interesting:

> This cure is effected by a succession of acts all suited to stir up a lively expectation of a blessing. The man was deaf and could not be spoken to. Jesus speaks in signs: (1) takes him aside from the multitude—*alone with Jesus*; (2) puts his fingers in his ears—*these are to be opened*; (3) touched his tongue with his saliva—*Christ's tongue is to heal his*; (4) looked up to heaven and sighed—*God's help in man's sorrow*; (5) spoke the word *Ephphatha*—and the man spoke plainly.'[1]

[1] T. M. Lindsay, *St. Mark*, p. 144.

31. Follow the R.V. here: 'And he again went out from the borders of Tyre, and came through Sidon to the sea of Galilee, through the midst of the borders of Decapolis.'

32. Had an impediment in his speech
Some think the man was a deaf mute, but the Greek word *mogilalos*, which means 'one speaking with difficulty' and v. 35 (HE SPAKE PLAIN, i.e. 'correctly'), both confirm the A.V. translation.

34. He sighed
Or groaned. The sighing of Christ's spirit in fervent prayer. Cf. Rom. 8. 26: 'The Spirit itself maketh intercessions for us with groanings that cannot be uttered.' EPHPHATHA. Like ABBA and TALITHA KUMI, one of the actual Aramaic words which Christ used.

37. Probably means: 'How well he fulfils the prophecy of Isaiah!'

> The ears of the deaf shall be unstopped . . .
> And the tongue of the dumb shall sing (35. 5 f.).

VIII

THE FEEDING OF THE FOUR THOUSAND

VIII. 1-10

(MATT. 15. 32-39)

THIS is either a variant account of the Feeding of the Five Thousand in Mark 6, or the account of a closely similar episode. (In favour of the former view is 8. 4, a question which is hard to understand if Jesus had in fact already fed a multitude in the desert. If this view be accepted, we may suppose that the first account came to Mark from Peter; the second from somebody else. On the other hand, the differences between the two stories—seven loaves instead of five, 4,000 people instead of 5,000—would support the second view.) In either case, separate treatment is not necessary.

8. Seven baskets

Not *kophinos*, as in the Feeding of the Five Thousand, but *spuris*, a hamper, is the word used here. It was in a *spuris* that Paul made his dramatic 'get-away' from Damascus (Acts 9. 25).

10. Dalmanutha

Is unknown. Is it a corruption of *Magdalutha*, and did it lie near Magdala on the west side of the lake?

THE DEMAND FOR A SIGN

8. 11-13 (Matt. 16. 1, 4)

'Jews ask for signs, and Greeks seek after wisdom,' said St. Paul. The Pharisees in this incident ran true to type. What they wished Jesus to produce was a sign with a capital S—a thaumaturgical *tour de force*—some audible or visible manifestation of overmastering power which would write the truth of Christ's claims plain across the sky. But, as in the wilderness he had renounced the temptation to dazzle the people into belief, so now he flatly refused any such sign.

Observe that Q also preserves a reference to the demand for a sign (see Luke 11. 29 f.; Matt. 12. 38 f.). On that occasion the only sign Jesus offered them was 'the sign of Jonah', i.e. the sign which consisted in himself and his message—God speaking to this generation through Jesus, as of old he spoke through Jonah to the Ninevites. On the other hand it was true that Jesus' miracles were signs—but only to those who had their spiritual eyes open to see the Reign of God present in Jesus and his ministry (Luke 10. 23 f.; Matt. 13. 16 f.).

The demand for a sign was not confined to the Pharisees of Jesus' day. When Thomas Carlyle said of God, 'He does nothing', he was in effect asking for a sign. God does not pander to this bit of the Jew in us. Yet he gives us signs every day and everywhere in his created world, and once in history he gave us a supreme sign—the sign of the crucified Jesus, who is 'the power and wisdom of God' for those who can read the sign:

> One Kingdom only is divine,
>   One banner triumphs still;
> Its King a servant, and its sign
>   A gibbet on a hill.[1]

---

[1] From 'In Hoc Signo' in *Through the Christian Year* (Bradby & Hunkin), p. 11.

ON BREAD AND BELIEVING

8. 14-21 (Matt. 16. 5-12)

Much of the difficulty of this section vanishes when we realise that v. 15, though a genuine saying of Jesus, is here out of its context. 'A modern writer,' says Turner, 'would have put it in a note at the foot of the page.'[1] If, then, we examine it separately, what does it mean? Leaven is often a metaphor for a bad influence, and so it must be here. Now, on the previous occasion when Herodians and Pharisees are mentioned together (3. 6), we find them making common cause to destroy Jesus. Probably, therefore, here 'the leaven of the Pharisees and of Herod' is their veiled hostility to Jesus and his mission. What Jesus says is: 'When you see Herod and the Pharisees getting together, then look out for trouble!'

Now for the rest. In the haste of their departure the disciples had forgotten to provision the boat. When they begin to worry about 'what they shall eat', Jesus reproaches them for their spiritual obtuseness. 'Have you no eyes to see? No ears to hear? No memories? Have you forgotten that I fed a multitude? Will you not realise that your Master is sufficient for every emergency?'

16. Follow the R.V.: 'And they reasoned one with another, saying, We have no bread.'

17. Hardened (dulled)

19 f. These verses imply *two* feeding miracles.

THE BLIND MAN OF BETHSAIDA

8. 22-26 (found in Mark only)

Bethsaida, the scene of this cure, was in the tetrarchy of Herod Philip, who had given it the name of Bethsaida Julias in honour of Augustus's daughter Julia. It was a considerable town, standing about a mile back from the north-east corner of the lake.

To avoid publicity, Jesus leads the blind man outside the

[1] *St. Mark*, p. 39.

town and, applying spittle to his eyes (it was commonly supposed to have therapeutic properties), and laying his hands on them, begins the cure: 'Do you see anything?' he asks. The reply is very vivid: 'I see men like trees, walking.' (Very similar were the words of a young American who, born without pupils, had his sight restored by a surgeon in 1931. The blind man of Bethsaida saw the human forms, larger than nature to his dazed vision—like tree trunks, only in motion. Who could have told this story to Mark but an eyewitness like Peter?) Again Jesus lays his hands on the man's eyes. And this time he is able to focus properly and to see everything 'distinctly' (*telaugōs*). Before the crowds can gather, Jesus sends the man to his home, which was evidently not in the village, with the admonition: 'Do not tell it even in the village.'

23. If he saw ought
Better, 'Do you see anything (*ei ti blepeis*)?'

26. Neither go . . . in the town
The probable text here is: 'Do not tell it even in the village.'[1]

PETER'S CONFESSION: THE MESSIAH AND THE CROSS

8. 27-33 (Matt. 16. 13-23; Luke 9. 18-22)

'This section is the turning-point in the Gospel. The Messianic Secret is out—but Messiahship means suffering, and the call to follow Christ means the fellowship of his sufferings.'

First, let us note the scene. Caesarea Philippi was an ancient town twenty-five miles north of Bethsaida, situated in a region of deep solitude and romantic beauty and almost in the shadow of snow-crowned Hermon. It lay in the tetrarchy of Herod Philip, who had rebuilt and renamed it after the Roman emperor. (Philip's Caesarea is to be distinguished from maritime Caesarea, where St. Paul lay two years in prison.)

[1] Turner, *op. cit.*, p. 39.

Somewhere in this region Jesus put the great Christo-logical question to the Twelve. For months he had laboured to *live it in upon them*, but he had never said plainly, 'I am the Messiah'. Now, in order that he might prepare them for a still more shattering revelation, he deliberately elicited from them an answer to his question 'Who do men say that I am?' They replied that all were agreed that he was someone with a divine commission, though popular opinion took different forms: the Baptist risen from the dead, or Elijah, or one of the ancient prophets. Then Jesus pressed the ques-tion down on them squarely: 'But you—who do you say that I am?' The answer was critical for Jesus as well as for the Twelve. If they had penetrated no more deeply than the people generally, he must still have stayed his advance. But Peter at once spoke out the thought that was in all their minds: 'You are the Messiah.' (Matthew adds 'the Son of the living God', and Luke has 'the Messiah of God'.) The Messiah was the heaven-sent Deliverer for whom the Jews had been waiting for centuries. Doubtless there were many and various dreams of the Coming One, as they called him; but the essential thing in every picture or dream of the Mes-siah was that he should be the Head of the People of God and the Bearer of God's Rule to men. He was the person in whom all God's saving purposes should be consummated. When Peter confessed Jesus to be the Messiah, he meant all that—he was giving him the highest title that any Jew could give him.

The confession elicited, Jesus at once commanded silence on the Twelve. Messiah he was, but such a Messiah as no Jew had ever before conceived. For, as he proceeded to tell them, 'The Son of Man *must* suffer many things. . . .' Note that 'must'. It is the 'must' of divine necessity. Jesus means that God's will for him points that way—points to suffering and death; and if we ask where Jesus found God's will revealed for him, there can be little doubt that he is thinking of the Suffering Servant of the Lord depicted in Isa. 53. This, then, was the staggering disclosure for which Jesus was preparing his disciples—the disclosure of a Mes-siah who must go to his glory by way of a cross. The central point of this story is not the disciples' realisation of Jesus' Messiahship. That, of course, was of capital importance, but it was only a preliminary—a necessary preliminary to the disclosure of the doctrine of the Cross. 'Jesus,' says Goguel finely, 'did not believe himself to be the Messiah *although* he had to suffer; he felt himself to be the Messiah *because* he had to suffer. There is the great paradox, the great originality of his Gospel.'[1]

However, the paradox of a suffering Messiah swept Peter out of his spiritual depth; he reproved Jesus only to be in turn reproved with terrible severity: 'Get behind me, you Satan! Your outlook is not God's but man's' (Moffatt). As Jesus listened to Peter's protest, his conflict in the wilderness came back to him in all its grim reality. Satan was speaking to him through Peter's lips, tempting him to follow a worldly course, tempting him to a saviourhood without a cross.

29. The Christ

CHRIST (*Christos*) is the Greek equivalent of the Hebrew Messiah.

31. Note that Jesus predicts not only his death, but also his resurrection. This is the first of three solemn predictions of his passion and triumph. AFTER THREE DAYS. In popular speech this phrase meant the same thing as 'on the third day', the phrase used by Matthew and Luke.

THE WAY OF DISCIPLESHIP

8. 34—9. 1 (Matt. 16. 24-28; Luke 9. 23-27)

Mark now gives us half a dozen sayings which Jesus spoke to his disciples on the theme of discipleship. (Most of them have their parallels in Q.) If nowadays we generalise them, we must remember that originally they were addressed to a few special men in a particular situation—men who were, in fact, just beginning the road that was to lead to a cross.

[1] Maurice Goguel, *Life of Jesus*, p. 392.

34. The people

If we are rather surprised to find them mentioned here, we must remember that 'any visitor with anything to say quickly draws a crowd in any Syrian village to-day'.[1] WHO-SOEVER WILL COME AFTER ME, etc. For us the Cross is a precious symbol of redemption. It requires real historical imagination to feel the sinister ring of these words as the disciples must have heard them. 'If you want to be my disciples,' Jesus says in effect, 'you must begin to live as men on their way to the gallows.' TO DENY HIMSELF means not to deny oneself something (as when we speak of 'self-denial'), but to 'renounce self'. It is the self-renunciation of the true missionary, one who like Paul 'counts not life dear'—a glad St. Francis, Livingstone or Schweitzer.

35. One of Jesus' great paradoxes. 'On the high emprise on which we are now embarked' is the meaning 'any man who puts self-preservation first will make shipwreck (we think of Judas), but he who gives up all for my sake and the Gospel's will win life eternal'. Cf. Luke 17. 33; Matt. 10. 39 (Q); and John 12. 25.

36. This is the Parable of the Rich Fool (Luke 12. 16-21) in a nutshell. The WORLD here denotes 'the glittering prizes' it has to offer—its pelf and power. To gain all these and to lose the supreme thing—life eternal now offered in Jesus and the Kingdom—were a bad business indeed. SOUL. Better, with the R.V., 'life'. The Greek word *psyche* should always in Mark (save in the two O.T. quotations 12. 30 and 14. 34) be rendered 'life'. ／

38. Disloyalty to Christ and its awful consequences here-after. The Q version of this saying should be carefully noted:

He who denies me before men shall be denied before the angels of God (Luke 12. 9).

Whosoever shall deny me before men, him will I also deny before my Father which is in heaven' (Matt. 10. 33).

F. C. Burkitt. *Jesus Christ*. p. 27.

In the Q version (which is probably more original) there is no reference to a 'coming' of Christ. Jesus says that a man who disowns him (in this world) will be disowned by him when they stand face to face before God in the unseen world. Stern words, not to be glossed over. On a man's attitude to Jesus will depend his eternal destiny. ADULTEROUS in the prophetic sense of 'apostate'.

9. 1. Some of those listening to him, says Jesus, will not experience death till they see God's Rule (already present in Jesus and his mission) COME WITH POWER (literally, in, or with, a miracle), i.e. signally and triumphantly—a prophecy which came true in the Resurrection, the Gift of the Spirit, and the victorious expansion of the Church after Pentecost. Similarly, in Rom. 1. 4, Paul says that Jesus was 'marked out' as the Son of God *with power* by the resurrection from the dead. Note how Matthew (16. 27 f.) has re-written this saying and made it refer to the Second Advent.

IX

THE TRANSFIGURATION

IX. 2-8

(MATT. 17. 1-8; LUKE 9. 28-36)

N.B.—The Lucan account has several very interesting additions to the Marcan story.

A WEEK after Peter's confession came the Transfiguration, probably on a spur of Mount Hermon. How are we to think of this strange, other-worldly story?

There are two initial points to be kept in mind. First, it is best to regard the narrative as the record of a *vision*, as indeed Matthew (17. 9) calls it. Second, the story is told from the point of view of the disciples. We may regard the Transfiguration as the *counterpart in the disciples' experience of the Baptism in the experience of our Lord*. (1) Both events concern revelations of Jesus' Messiahship; (2) in both, the secret is revealed by a vision and a voice; (3) the words of the voice are in both cases very similar. Keeping these points in mind, we may now try to ask and answer three questions: (1) What happened to our Lord? (2) What was the experience of the disciples? (3) Was the vision genuine?

The answer to the first question is that we know very little about Jesus' experience on this occasion. It is not only that we cannot penetrate far into the religious experience of our Lord, but we cannot appraise with any scientific precision the strange sight which the three disciples saw as they watched their Master rapt in prayer. All we can say is that

Jesus went through an experience of self-dedication to his
Father's will as he now saw it clearly in all its sombre significance (cf. Luke 9. 31: 'They spake of his *exodus* which
he was about to accomplish at Jerusalem'). We need only
add that there are recorded observations of a luminous glow
transfiguring the faces of saints in prayer.

What of the disciples' experience? It was only a week after
Peter's confession. They knew that he was the Messiah, but
along with that disclosure had come another still more startling—the doctrine of the Cross. If, in one way, the mystery
of Jesus' person had been illumined for them, in another
way it had been deepened and intensified. The disciples were
in a state of tension. They were also (as Luke tells us) 'heavy
with sleep'. May we not say that an imaginative release of
this tension was inevitable, and that it expressed itself in
vision and audition? In this vision and audition the imaginative material in their minds—their conviction of Jesus' Messiahship, his place in the divine economy of history, his
relation to the Law (Moses) and the Prophets (Elijah)—was
projected outwards. They saw Moses and Elijah with Jesus.
They heard a divine endorsement of Jesus' claim.

Was the vision genuine? And, if it was, what did it signify?
The criterion of the genuineness of any vision is not in its
form, but in its spiritual content. That this was a genuine,
a divinely caused vision, no Christian will doubt. In it God
set the seal on Peter's confession and convinced them of its
truth.

2. Peter, James and John
The inner circle again. AN HIGH MOUNTAIN. Traditionally,
Mount Tabor; more probably, Hermon. 5. THREE TABER-
NACLES or booths. Peter wished to keep the heavenly visi-
tants. 7. THIS IS MY BELOVED SON. Compare the voice at the
Baptism.

A DIFFICULTY ABOUT ELIJAH
9. 9-13 (Matt. 17. 9-13)

These verses are difficult until one sees that there has been
a little displacement. If we put 12b after 10, all becomes

clear. What the disciples discussed was (1) what rising from
the dead meant, and (2) how it could be written in scripture
that the Son of Man must suffer many things (i.e. they were
wrestling with the problem of a Suffering Messiah). To the
disciples' question, Why do the scribes say that Elijah must
first come? Jesus replies, 'True, but I tell you that Elijah
has already come (in the person of John the Baptist, who
was the Forerunner) and they have served him as scripture
said they would'. John had found his Jezebel in Herodias
(cf. 1 Kings 19. 2, 10).

10. If Jesus had said simply, 'till Resurrection Day' (i.e. the
great eschatological event), the disciples would not have been
puzzled. What puzzled them was this saying about the Son
of Man rising from the dead; for they had no place in their
theology for a dying Messiah.

THE EPILEPTIC BOY
9. 14-29 (Matt. 17. 14-21; Luke 9. 37-43a)

From the majestic beauty of the scene on the mount we
pass to the piteous spectacle of human misery presented by
the epileptic boy. The boy's symptoms are clearly those of
an epileptic, with a tendency to suicidal mania. Before this
case the nine disciples are helpless, as the father of the boy
explains from the edge of the crowd. With a sigh for this
generation's faithlessness, Jesus summons the lad to him.
Apparently the sight of Jesus produces another convulsion.
When our Lord asks, 'How long has he been like this?' the
father answers, 'Since childhood. But if you have any power,
for pity's sake help me'. 'If you have any power,' Jesus
repeats. 'All things are in the power of him who has faith!'
(That is, a man with real faith will refuse to set limits to
God's power present in Jesus.) Whereupon the father replies,
'Sir, I do have faith—if it is not enough, do you help me'
(i.e. help me to increase it—itself a noble confession of
faith). Jesus utters a command: 'It is I who command you,
Come out!' There is another convulsion which leaves the
boy like a corpse. Then the Lord takes him by the hand, and
he gets up.

Afterwards, in private, the disciples ask: 'Why could not we expel the offending spirit?' 'This sort,' answers Jesus, 'will yield only to prayer.' The disciples had either not prayed, or had not prayed enough about the case. (The words AND FASTING found in the A.V. are probably a scribe's gloss, and should be omitted.) Once again we note the tremendous emphasis which Jesus lays on faith and on prayer as the means to it. If we had more of 'the faith that rebels', the faith that refuses to acquiesce in accepted views of what is possible and impossible, the faith that expects great things from God as its birthright, we should not only find our Lord's miracles more credible, but we should find for ourselves a power-house of illimitable energy.

18. pineth away

The Greek verb (*xerainetai*) should be rendered 'becomes rigid': the sign of an epileptic fit.

19. How long shall I be with you?

'A cry of homesickness—as though Jesus had a profound nostalgia for his heavenly Father' (Lowrie).

SECOND PREDICTION OF THE PASSION
9. 30-32 (Matt. 17. 22-23; Luke 9. 43b-45)

From the neighbourhood of Mount Hermon Jesus now moves south, through Galilee, with Jerusalem as his goal. He goes as quietly as he can, partly because he wishes to escape the notice of Herod Antipas, partly because he wishes to prepare the Twelve for the Cross and all that lies beyond it. Once more he forecasts his passion and resurrection: 'The Son of Man is being delivered up into the hands of men. The Greek verb for DELIVERED (*paradidotai*) implies that it was by the Father's hand that his surrender was being made into the hands of men. 'He that spared not his own Son,' said Paul later, looking back on the finished work, 'but *delivered him up* for us all' (Rom. 8. 32). But the Twelve found the saying a tragic puzzle; and, possibly remembering Jesus' rebuke of Peter, feared to interrogate him further.

TRUE GREATNESS
9. 33-37 (Matt. 18. 1-5; Luke 9. 46-48)

On the dusty road to Capernaum the Twelve were dis-
cussing greatness and, in particular, who was the greatest in
the disciple band. Jesus overheard their discussion, but said
nothing about it till they went 'indoors'. 'What were you
talking about out there on the road?' he asked. There was
an uncomfortable silence. Assuming the teacher's sitting
posture, Jesus called the Twelve around him. 'Greatness,'
he taught them, 'greatness in the Kingdom is something
utterly different from what the world counts greatness. The
first man in my Father's Kingdom is he who is ready to be
last, who is ready to be the slave of all. True greatness is
service; service is true greatness.'

There followed a simple 'action-sermon'. Setting a child
in the disciples' midst, he 'put his arms around him', saying:
'He who welcomes a little one like this for my sake, welcomes me, and he who welcomes me welcomes my Father
whose ambassador I am.'

This saying, with Jesus' other sayings about children, has
had an influence for good in the world past all calculation.
Says Montefiore the Jew: 'Who can measure or count the
deeds of sacrifice and love to which this saying has promp-
ed? Wherever Christian men and women have sought to
cherish and save helpless little children, we can almost hear
the echoes of this saying.'[1] And if to-day men show a solicitude for little children that would have amazed the ancients,
that solicitude takes its origin from one Man.

37. Observe Jesus' claim to be God's accredited envoy to
men. This saying has a parallel in Q (Luke 10. 16; Matt.
10. 40).

N.B.—With this story compare the similar one in 10. 13-
16. The curious thing is that the saying in 9. 37 is more
appropriate to the second story, as the saying in 10. 15 is to
the first one. For 'when the Twelve have been coveting posi-
tions of greatness above one another, it seems more in point

[1] C. G. Montefiore, *The Synoptic Gospels*, i, p. 229.

to speak of the duty of receiving the Kingdom of God in a
childlike spirit than to speak of receiving the children; and,
conversely, when the disciples have done their best to prevent
access of the children to Christ, the duty of receiving such
children in his name looks to be the more natural comment'.[1]
It looks as if Mark has misplaced the two sayings.

A LESSON IN TOLERANCE
9. 38-40 (Luke 9. 49-50)

The reference to the 'name' of Jesus recalls another occasion when the 'name' had been in question: the case of the
strange exorcist. The historical setting of this episode is obviously a time when the Twelve were separated from Jesus;
and we may hazard the guess that it is a reminiscence from
the Mission of the Twelve. One day John and his co-
missioner had overheard a rival exorcist using their Master's
name in his professional formula (cf. the sons of Sceva in
Acts 19. 13 ff.). 'We tried to stop him,' John said, 'because
he was not one of your professing followers.' 'Never do
that,' replies Jesus, 'no one can do a mighty work in my
name and easily speak evil of me.' The saying commands
tolerance towards those who act in Christ's name, even although they are not Church members. It is capable of wide
application. There are many who do the Lord's work, though
they do not belong to his outward fellowship or openly
admit that they are Christians. Zealous Christians must beware of hindering their good work.

40. For he that is not against us is on our part

Better, 'for us'. But does not Jesus say elsewhere (Luke
11. 23; Matt. 12. 30): 'He that is not with me is against me'?
Is there not here a flagrant contradiction? The answer is that
interpretation must always take account of context. In this
second case the context is one of active hostility against
Jesus. In such circumstances, Jesus says, neutrality is tanta-
mount to hostility (as Pilate, at the trial, electing to play the
role of the great neutral, helped to send Jesus to the Cross).

[1] Turner, *op. cit.*, p. 48.

OBITER DICTA TO THE DISCIPLES

9. 41-50 (Matt. 18. 6-9; Luke 17. 1 f. Vv. 44, 46, and 49b in Mark are
no part of the true text)

The verses contain sayings of Jesus to the disciples on various topics—service, snares, salt.

41. Omit in my name
Whoever shows the smallest kindness to one of the disciples, because he is a disciple of Christ, will be rewarded by God. Our Lord is clearly looking into the future when the disciples will be preaching the Gospel of Christ (cf. Matt. 10. 42).

42. Conversely, the man who 'offends', i.e. leads astray, the humblest believer in Christ were better drowned like a dog (cf. Luke 17. 1 f.). Stern words. It is no light thing to trifle with any man's faith in Christ.

43, 45, 47, 48. From offences against others Jesus turns to offences that concern one's own self. Everything which imperils a man's chance of Life or the Kingdom (they are both synonyms for salvation) must be ruthlessly renounced. Better to be saved, though you lose something precious in the process, than to go to perdition with all your advantages. HELL is literally 'Gehenna'. The valley of Hinnom near Jerusalem was the place where refuse was burnt. It became a symbol for future punishment, so that our 'hell' is a proper enough translation. Whether we like it or not, Jesus did so put the alternatives—Life or perdition. But he did not, of course, dwell with relish (as sometimes his followers have done) on the pains awaiting the lost in the next world.

48. Cf. Isa. 66. 24.

49-50. The section ends with three sayings on salt. In the first, Jesus seems to warn the disciples that they must be purified by trials (cf. 1 Cor. 3. 13). In the second, which is another version of the saying preserved in Matt. 5. 13 (Luke 14. 34 f., Q), he tells them that a disciple who had lost his zeal and devotion is like salt that has gone insipid. Since salt was a symbol of friendship or concord (the Arabs say, 'There is salt between us'), the third saying must mean 'Keep your fellowship whole and intact', perhaps a reference back to their quarrelling.

X

THE QUESTION OF DIVORCE

X. 1-12

(MATT. 19. 1-12; 5. 31 f.; cf. LUKE 16. 18)

THE scene now moves across the Jordan to the district known as Perea. Jesus resumes teaching, and some Pharisees ask his opinion on the question of divorce, a question much debated at that time. One rabbinical school (that of Hillel) held that a husband could divorce his wife for no more serious misconduct than 'letting his food burn'. Another (that of Shammai) allowed divorce only for unchastity (cf. Matt. 19. 9 and 5. 32). Both these views were interpretations of Deut. 24. 1 f. (especially the italicised clause):

> When a man taketh a wife and marrieth her, then it shall be that if she find no favour in his eyes, *because he hath found some unseemly thing in her*, that he shall write her a bill of divorcement, and give it in her hand, and send her out of his house.

Jesus, as often, answers first with a question. 'What did Moses (i.e. Deuteronomy) command?' 'Moses,' they reply, 'permitted divorce, providing, however, that the husband should give his wife a certificate of divorce.' Thereupon Jesus sweeps aside not only the Rabbis' interpretations, but the actual text of Deut. 24. 1 f. 'Moses' directive,' he says in effect, 'was simply an accommodation to human weakness. It violates the divine ideal of marriage.' And he quotes Gen.

1. 27 and 2. 24 in proof. 'What,' he asks, 'was God's purpose in instituting marriage? Surely it was that of a lifelong
union whose claims take precedence over those of parents.'

Afterwards, privately, the disciples ask Jesus to amplify
his answer. To appreciate his explanation in v. 11, we must
recall that in Jewish law, while a woman could commit
adultery against her husband, a husband could not commit
adultery against his wife. The new feature in Jesus' reply is
his declaration that a husband can commit adultery against
his wife.

One point more. The so-called 'excepting clause' found
in Matt. 5. 32 and 19. 9, represents the mind, not of Jesus,
but of a section of the early Church who shrank from the
rigour (as some of us do) of Christ's ruling. Its effect is to
make Jesus take sides with the school of Shammai. Our
Lord made no such exception. For him, marriage was an
indissoluble bond. So long as flesh and blood endure, man
and wife are ideally inseparable. 'It is a quite irrefragable
conclusion,' says C. H. Turner, 'that our Lord absolutely
excluded divorce from the Christian code.'[1] Paul knew this
Dominical ruling (cf. 1 Cor. 7. 10).

1. Coasts
Better, 'region'. The region 'beyond Jordan' is Perea. What
Mark means here is that they now turned their steps towards Judea in the south, and to get there followed the route
through Perea on the east side of Jordan.

6. From the beginning of the creation
The Greek ap' archēs ktiseōs probably renders the Hebrew
of Gen. 1. 1 Bereshith baɪa, meaning 'In the (Genesis)
creation passage'. Compare 'in the bush' (12. 26).

11. Against her
Against the first wife.

12.
This verse seems to contradict the Jewish law that a wife
could not divorce her husband. If so, it may be that what
Jesus said is to be found in Luke 16. 18. But there is some

[1] Turner, op. cit., p. 48.

evidence that divorce of the husband by the wife was a legal possibility.

THE BLESSING OF THE CHILDREN

10. 13-16 (Matt. 19. 13-15; Luke 18. 15-17)

The mothers bring their children to get the great Rabbi's touch and blessing. But the disciples would spare Jesus their attentions, much as a celebrity's supporters to-day might try to rescue him from the importunities of autograph hunters. 'Jesus became indignant' (*eganaktēse*): 'Let the children come to me! Stop preventing them. For to such belongs the Kingdom of God. I tell you truly, whoever does not receive the Kingdom of God as a child shall not enter it.'

Obviously Jesus treats the children not as citizens, but as *symbols* of the Kingdom. But what sort of childlikeness is necessary for the Kingdom? Not innocence, surely, as we sometimes imagine. For Jesus came to save sinners, not innocents; and moreover, whatever fond parents may think, any nursemaid knows that little children are not 'little innocents'. It is the *relation* of the child that is in Christ's mind. Whether it be an attractive child or not, a child it is, and entirely dependent on its parents. Everything comes from them—is their gift. The child's part is to receive—to take and not to earn. So it is not the innocence of the child but its receptiveness that is the point here. Unless we are prepared to receive God's Kingdom (or salvation) as a child receives a gift at his father's hand, we shall not have it. It is a parable of pure grace. And men still receive God's Kingdom as little children. The Kingdom of our Father is not for the proud and self-sufficient, but for those who, owning their weakness, cast themselves on God's grace and mercy made available for them in Christ.

Why was infant baptism received almost without a whisper of dissension in the early Church? Surely because all recognised it to be a custom entirely consonant with the mind of Christ. If we seek Dominical sanction for our practice, what better warrant have we than this moving story?

16. And he took them up in his arms

A lovely detail preserved by Mark alone. It scandalised the other two evangelists, who left it out.

THE RICH YOUNG RULER

10. 17-22 (Matt. 19. 16-22; Luke 18. 18-23)

(Note that the traditional title is composite. 'Rich' is from Mark 10. 22, 'young' from Matt. 19. 20, and 'ruler' from Luke 18. 18.)

Out on the road again they encounter a man who runs to Jesus, kneels, and asks: 'Good Master, what must I do to inherit eternal life?' At once Jesus cross-examines him on his use of terms: 'Why do you call me good? Only one person is good—God.' Does this question betray, as some have held, a consciousness of sin in Jesus?[1] (cf. Matt. 19. 17). But Jesus does not say 'I am not good'. He says: 'Why do you call me good? Goodness exists only in God.' That is, are your words only a conventional flattery (like our 'Right Honourable', sometimes, in the House!) or do you perceive that my goodness can have only one source, God? 'It is,' says Calvin, 'as if he said: ''Thou falsely callest me Good Master unless thou acknowledgest that I come from God''.'[2]

Then Jesus continues: 'You know the commandments', and he cites the fifth, sixth, seventh, eighth, and ninth, plus 'Do not defraud'. The man replies that he has kept all these since boyhood. Jesus at once 'took a liking to him'. Discerning great possibilities in him, he put him to the test. 'You lack one thing. Go, sell all your possessions, give the proceeds to the poor, and then follow me.' But the man failed at the test. Jesus had diagnosed his weakness. His wealth stood between him and full surrender to Christ. '*With a lowering face* at the word' (this is the meaning of the Greek *stugnasas*) he departed sorrowfully. We cannot help thinking of another young man who could also say: 'All these have I kept since my youth up' (see Phil. 3. 6), but who, when the chance offered, was not afraid to 'count all loss for Christ'.

---

[1] Wellhausen says 'good' (*agathos*) means 'kindly'.
[2] Quoted by T. M. Lindsay, *op. cit.*, on this passage.

19. Defraud not

Probably Mark's version of the tenth commandment, 'which
was originally aimed against greedy desire for another's
goods which led to oppressions and cheating'.[1]

21. Omit the words 'Take up thy cross'. Jesus' command to
this man does not mean that absolute renunciation of wealth
is a necessary condition of all Christian discipleship. This
was not a rule for all Christians, but a prescription for a
particular case.

THE DANGER OF RICHES
10. 23-31 (Matt. 19. 23-30; Luke 18. 24-30)

These sayings on the spiritual peril of riches follow natur
ally on the great refusal. The disciples had just seen a mar-
refuse the pearl of great price because he could not bring
himself to part with his wealth. Jesus comments sadly: 'How
hardly shall they that have riches enter into the Kingdom of
God!' Yet his liking for this young man had not made him
abate one jot of the law which he enunciated elsewhere: 'Ye
cannot serve God and Mammon.' The rigour of his doctrine
staggers the disciples. 'If this is so,' they remonstrate, 'who
on earth has any chance of being saved?' (Observe in this
context that to 'enter the Kingdom' is equivalent to 'being
saved'.) Jesus' reply is that God of his grace and power can
do what is seemingly impossible. Whereupon, his hope re-
viving a little, Peter asks: 'Will what we have done (renounced everything for your sake) secure us a place in the
Kingdom?' 'Everyone,' replies Jesus, 'who has sacrificed
home ties for my sake and the Gospel's will gain manifold
new ties—"mothers" in every Christian matron, "children" in every Christian family, and "homes" in every
Christian household—in this present life, WITH PERSECU-
TIONS [Jesus holds out no rose-coloured prospect for his
followers this side of eternity]—AND IN THE WORLD TO COME,
ETERNAL LIFE.'

Christians still find these sayings of Christ about riches

[1] A. H. MacNeile, *Exodus*, p. 121.

'hard'. While we dare not say that no rich man will be saved, we must not blind ourselves to the stark, uncomfortable truth that the love of money does most effectively disable a man for the Kingdom. It was so then; it is so still.

24. The words 'for them that trust in riches', not found in the best MSS., should be omitted.

25. There is no evidence for the widely current view that a small gate in Jerusalem bore the name 'Needle's Eye'. That gate exists, as Rawlinson says, only in the imagination of Jerusalem guides![1] The figure of the camel and the needle's eye is a picturesque hyperbole for the well-nigh impossible.

30. For an illustration of 'mothers' see Rom. 16. 13.

31. A maxim of Christ's repeated elsewhere. In the realm of God human values and valuations are reversed. The Beatitudes emphasise the same truth. So do the careers of Judas and Paul.

THE THIRD PREDICTION OF THE PASSION
10. 32-34 (Matt. 20. 17-19; Luke 18. 31-34)

With this section we are made to feel that the climax to the Gospel story is approaching. Somewhere on the road to Jerusalem Jesus for the third time predicts his passion and resurrection (cf. 8. 31 and 9. 31). Verse 32, one of the most wonderful in the Gospels, is more accurately translated in the R.V. 'And they were in the way, going up to Jerusalem; and Jesus was going before them: and they were amazed; and they that followed were afraid'. We are to picture two parties —Jesus a great lonely figure striding ahead; and the disciples following, awe-stricken, at a distance. What AMAZED them was the kind of lead which Jesus had taken. Never before had he so stepped out ahead of them, as though impatiently eager to be at the goal of his journey. He was wholly absorbed in something that passed the wit of the disciples. And if we ask what that thing was, there can be only one answer. Jesus (as Bengel says) 'was already dwelling in his passion'.

[1] *St. Mark*, p. 72.

32. And he took again the twelve

Took them up again into company with him; and as soon as they were level with him, spoke with them on the subject that lay heavy on his soul. Some of the words of this third prediction may have been made more precise in the light of what actually happened; but there is no reason for denying that the substance of the prediction is authentic.

THE REQUEST OF JAMES AND JOHN

10. 35-45 (Matt. 20. 20-28) (Luke omits the request of James and John and places the dispute about the precedence in the context of the Last Supper. See Luke 22. 24-27)

To understand this request we may recall that in the difficult saying about 'the twelve thrones' (Matt. 19. 28; Luke 22. 30) Jesus had promised the disciples a position of privilege in the heavenly Kingdom. Now the sons of Zebedee, not content with the promise, wish Jesus to assure them of the two chief places in it. 'You do not know what you are requesting,' replies Jesus sadly; 'what my glory is, and what is required of those who shall sit there. Can you brace yourselves to undergo the awful ordeal I am undergoing?' When they reply 'We can', Jesus takes them at their word; they will endure suffering (was not James eventually martyred? Acts 12. 2); but the gift of the chief places is in his Father's hand.

We may sympathise with the indignation of the Ten at the Two. Jesus praised neither Ten nor Two. With the sky lowering and Calvary ahead, they were still blinded by visions of thrones and crowns—by Gentile dreams of greatness. Not in the despotic exercise of power, but in humble service lay God's idea of greatness. For even the Son of Man—the very Vicegerent of God—came not to be served but to serve, and to give his life to redeem the many whose own lives had otherwise been forfeit.

38. Both CUP and BAPTISM are metaphors for his passion. In the Old Testament the 'cup' is often a symbol for a lot ordained by God, generally one of affliction. If we would define Christ's metaphor further, we may say, with Denney,[1] that it was 'the cup our sins had mingled' (cf. Mark 14. 36). BAPTISM signifies here 'being overwhelmed by calamity'. 'I have,' says Jesus in effect, 'deep waters to pass through' (cf. Luke 12. 50). 'The baptism by water was the initiation of the hidden Messiah, and the baptism of death was his initiation as the Lord of glory.'[2]

39. Observe how Jesus, despite their ignorance and wrong motives, took James and John at their word. 'Christ,' said George Macdonald, 'is easy to please, but hard to satisfy.' He accepts our miserable best, but on that he insists on building his own.

43. Cf. Luke 22. 27 and John 13. 1-20.

45. The great Ransom passage. It shows clearly how Jesus knew himself called to fuse in his own destiny the two roles of the Son of Man (Dan. 7) and the Servant of the Lord (Isa. 53). The word RANSOM (*lutron*), i.e. purchase price to free those in bondage, and the preposition FOR (*anti*, 'instead of'), imply that Jesus, as the Son of Man, is doing something for the many which they cannot do for themselves. What is it? 'At the very least we must infer that Christ's death takes the place of the many; and the natural interpretation is that the death of the innocent one exempts the guilty.'[3] THE MANY, a phrase taken from Isa. 53. 12, must include Gentiles as well as Jews. We may regard this saying as Christ's own answer to the question, 'Are there few that be saved?'

BARTIMAEUS

10. 46-52 (Matt. 20. 29-34; Luke 18. 35-43)

Another stage in the last journey—Jericho. It was usual for Galileans, on their way to Jerusalem, to avoid Samaria by taking the route on the east side of Jordan, which they re-crossed at a ford near Jericho. Luke 19. 1-10 records

[1] *The Death of Christ*, p. 64.
[2] Lowrie, *op. cit.*, p. 406.
[3] Campbell Moody, *The Purpose of Jesus*, p. 95.

another happening in Jericho (the episode of Zaccheus). As
Jesus and the disciples begin the fifteen miles uphill journey
to Jerusalem from Jericho, accompanied by A GREAT NUM-
BER OF PEOPLE (doubtless Galileans going up for the Passover), they pass the spot where a blind beggar had his 'pitch'.
Since he is named so circumstantially, Bartimaeus was probably well known in the Jerusalem Church. Clearly the Messianic secret had begun to leak out, for Bartimaeus hails
Jesus as 'Son of David', a Messianic title. If the crowd bade
him be quiet, it was not because they were concerned to keep
the Messianic secret, but because they wished Jesus' progress to be uninterrupted. Jesus no longer enjoined silence;
he accepted the naïve faith of the beggar and summoned
him. The response was instantaneous: we can almost see
Bartimaeus 'casting away his garment' (in order to run more
easily), springing up, and making his way to Jesus. Jesus
restored his sight. 'Thy faith hath made thee whole'; that is,
has cured thee. And Bartimaeus, who had done the best bit
of begging in his life, at once took his place in the procession
towards Jerusalem.

49. Be of good comfort

More simply, 'cheer up'.

51. Lord

The Greek word is *Rabboni*, a more respectful form of
Rabbi used by Mary Magdalene so movingly in the Garden
(John 20. 16). For 'Reverend Sir' Bartimaeus said, 'Very
Reverend Sir'.

XI

THE TRIUMPHAL ENTRY

XI. 1-11

(MATT. 21. 1-9; LUKE 19. 28-38; cf. JOHN 12. 12-19)

From this time onwards our Lord's acts are best understood in terms of 'prophetic symbolism'. Every reader of the Old Testament knows that the prophets often acted out their predictions. Thus, to take only one example, Jeremiah once solemnly broke an earthenware bottle before a group of his fellow countrymen in order to symbolise the 'breaking' of Jerusalem which he foretold (Jer. 19.).[1] The prophet's act was more than a vivid illustration of his words. In his action he conceived of himself as entering into the divine purpose and contributing to its fulfilment. To this category belong Christ's three actions during the last week in Jerusalem: the Triumphal Entry, the Cleansing of the Temple, and the Breaking of the Loaf at the Last Supper.

In Jesus' mind the Triumphal Entry was undoubtedly a piece of prophetic or (since he knew himself to be far more than a prophet) Messianic symbolism. Borrowing an ass from some staunch friend, probably in Bethphage ('the village over against you'), he rode the last two miles, via the Mount of Olives and across the brook Kidron, into the Holy City; while the disciples and the pilgrims coming up for the Passover spread their garments and branches in the way and chanted a Messianic greeting.

[1] Jer. 27. 2 and Ezek. 4. 1-3 provide further examples.

The clue to the meaning of Christ's action is in Zech. 9. 9 (quoted by Matthew and John). Centuries before, a seer had pictured the Messiah as 'lowly and riding upon an ass', adding that he would 'speak peace unto the nations' and 'his dominion would be from sea to sea'. This prophecy Jesus now deliberately acted out. By his action he proclaimed that he was the Messiah, but a Messiah contrary to all their dreaming, a Messiah without arms or an army, who was riding in lowly pomp that road of the spirit marked out for the Servant of the Lord, a road upon which ever darker fell the shadow of a cross.

1. Bethany
A village at the second milestone from Jerusalem. BETH-PHAGE was probably a little nearer. The Mount of Olives lies hardly more than half a mile from the city.

2 f. Obviously Jesus had some prearranged understanding with a friend in Bethphage.

3. And straightway he will send him hither
Better, 'and he (Jesus) will send him back here immediately'. A promise to return the ass as soon as it has served its purpose.

4. In a place where two ways met
Better, 'in the open street' (R.V.).

7. Cast their garments on him
To serve as a saddle for the 'unbroken' ass.

9 f. The salutation is based on Ps. 118. 25 f. HOSANNA = Heb. hōshă-nnā, i.e. 'save now'.
Since the words from Ps. 118 were the normal welcome given to the pilgrims (by the priests) as they arrived for the Feast, some have held that there was nothing Messianic about the ovation. But the second line of the greeting implies that the crowd, like Bartimaeus earlier in the day, saw in Jesus the Davidic Messiah. Quite probably this episode formed part of the charge later laid before Pilate (15. 3).

11. Jesus had travelled that day from Jericho to Jerusalem, after probably resting in Bethphage or Bethany. Evening was falling as he entered the Temple and saw the traffic there. What he saw made him resolve to act on the morrow.

HE WENT OUT UNTO BETHANY WITH THE TWELVE. Evidently, Jesus lodged from Sunday to Wednesday at Bethany. No doubt one reason was that the city was crowded and lodging scarce. But there was another. Had he stayed in the city he would have facilitated a premature *coup* by the authorities.

THE CURSING OF THE FIG TREE
11. 12-14 (Matt. 21. 18-19 (20-22))

This is one of the most perplexing stories in the Gospels, and Luke, who doubtless felt its difficulty, has left it out. What perplexes us is not so much the nature-miracle implied, as the unworthy light it casts on the character of Jesus. With our knowledge of Jesus from other sources, we find it frankly incredible that he could have used his power to wither a fig tree because it did not yield figs two or three months before its natural time of fruitage. Let those who will regard it as a 'miracle of judgment'; for ourselves, we must ask *Why* should Jesus work such a miracle?

Yet a core of history must underlie the story. Now Luke relates that Jesus once spoke a parable about a barren fig tree (Luke 13. 6-9). The fig tree was Israel, and in the parable Jesus said (in effect): 'You, my hearers, are in the same position as that fig tree.' With this clue to guide us we may guess that the kernel of Mark's story was not a miracle, but a parable of judgment. As Jesus once used a child to symbolise the Kingdom, so on the road to Jerusalem, finding a fig tree with leaves but no fruit, he drew from it a parable of the rejection of unfruitful Israel. Later, perhaps, the fig tree died; or maybe on the Jericho-Jerusalem road there was some conspicuous withered fig tree to which there became attached a story ascribing its cursing to Jesus.

13. For the time of figs was not yet

Figs do not ripen till June. This was the Passover time.

THE CLEANSING OF THE TEMPLE
11. 15-19 (Matt. 21. 12 f.; Luke 19. 45-48; cf. John 2. 13-17)

The second act of Messianic symbolism was the Cleansing of the Temple on the day after the Triumphal Entry. St. John places this episode at the beginning of Jesus' ministry; but it is far more appropriate in the context of the last week.

The scene was the Court of the Gentiles, the only place in the Temple area assigned to the Gentiles for prayer. This Annas and his Sadducean satellites had converted into a holy market where, at a profit to the priests, pilgrims could buy sacrificial victims (e.g. doves for purification, Luke 2. 24) and change their Gentile money into the Jewish coin required for the Temple dues. There, in a place which Jesus had once called 'My Father's House', he now found 'all the sweltering of a dirty cattle-market and the haggling of a dirtier exchange of money'. In the sheer strength of his heart's anger he swept it clean of its holy hucksters and stopped the right of way through the Temple courts. And to his action he added stinging words from the old prophets: 'My house shall be called a house of prayer for all nations (Isa. 56. 7), but you have made it a den of thieves' (Jer. 7. 11).

Yet we err if we see in Jesus' action only the indignation of a religious reformer. This was a *Messianic* act. It is hard to doubt that some words of Malachi were ringing in his head as he cleansed the Temple. 'The Lord whom ye seek shall suddenly come to his Temple, but who may abide the day of his coming? And he shall purify the sons of Levi, and purge them as gold and silver' (Mal. 3. 1 f.). The Cleansing was a symbol of the Lord coming in his Kingdom —a symbol proclaiming that the original purpose of God in ordaining worship in his house was to be honoured, and the People of God prepared for the advent of his Kingdom and Messiah.

No wonder THE SCRIBES AND CHIEF PRIESTS resolved to DESTROY HIM. The Temple Cleansing was both a challenge and a threat. Jesus threw down the gage to the authorities: he threatened both their prestige and their pockets.

16. Through the Temple

The Temple courts (like the nave of old St. Paul's, in London) were being used as a thoroughfare by business people.

17. Of all nations

Observe the universalism of Jesus. If we say it is unlikely Jesus stressed these words, must we not also say that he read Isaiah unsympathetically?

FAITH AND PRAYER

11. 20-25 (Matt. 21. 20-22)

After relating the sequel to the cursing of the fig tree, Mark records several sayings of our Lord on faith and prayer.

23. This saying on mountain-moving faith has a parallel in Q (Matt. 17. 20; Luke 17. 6). 'Moving a mountain' was a proverbial phrase for doing the apparently impossible.[1] Jesus means that a victorious faith can achieve almost anything. 'This word of Jesus does not invite Christians to become conjurers and magicians, but heroes like those whose exploits are celebrated in the eleventh chapter of Hebrews.'[2]

24. Receive

Read 'have received'. A more paradoxical form of 'Ask and it shall be given you'. It teaches the boundless possibilities of believing prayer.

25. Our forgiveness by God depends on our forgiving our fellow-men: the same thought as in the Lord's Prayer.

26. The R.V. omits this verse, which is obviously a scribe's insertion from Matt. 6. 15.

[1] Cf. 1 Cor. 13. 2. But it is just possible that the mountain-moving is Messianic and that we should compare Zech. 14. 4.
[2] T. W. Manson, *The Mission and Message of Jesus*, p. 433.

BY WHAT AUTHORITY?

11. 27-33 (Matt. 21. 23-27; Luke 20. 1-8)

Now follows a series of provocative questions (interrupted only by the Parable of the Wicked Husbandman) put to Jesus by his adversaries in an endeavour to trap him into some damaging admission: (1) By what authority? (2) May God's People pay tribute to a worldly State? (3) Do the dead rise? (4) What is the chief commandment?

The question 'By what authority doest thou these things?' arose naturally out ot the Temple Cleansing. It was asked by what looks like a deputation from the Sanhedrin. They wished him to justify his act, hoping doubtless that he would prematurely avow his Messiahship. Jesus adroitly evaded the trap by countering with another question, which we may paraphrase as 'Do you think God was behind John's mission or not?' This, observe, was more than a mere conundrum to 'fox' his adversaries. The question bore directly on he situation. John had pointed to Jesus as a greater than himself, for whom his work was but a preparation; if John's mission were from God, then Jesus' mission was from God also, and his Cleansing of the Temple an act well within his rights.

His adversaries were perplexed. If they said 'Of course, John was a man sent from God', Jesus could retort 'Then why did you pillars of the Church not believe in him?' If, however, they said that John's mission was a merely human affair, they had to reckon with the common people, who had no more doubt of the divinely inspired nature of John's mission than the people of France had of that of Joan of Arc. Jesus had won the first battle of wits.

27. The chief priests and the scribes and the elders

These were the constituent parts of the Jewish Sanhedrin or Council of Seventy.

XII

THE WICKED HUSBANDMEN
XII. 1-12
(MATT. 21. 33-46; LUKE 20. 9-19)

Having parried the question about authority, Jesus now told an allegory whose meaning must have been provocatively plain to his adversaries, for in it he denounced them beforehand as the murderers of the Messiah.

It is often said that the parables of Jesus are true parables (i.e. they contain only one point, and the details have no separate significance but serve only to enforce the main point). This is generally true; but Jesus could also use allegory, and the tale of the Wicked Husbandmen is a clear example. For this tale demands for its understanding that we make certain equations: the Vineyard—Israel; the Owner —God; the Husbandmen (or tenants)—the Jews; the servants—the Prophets; the only son and heir—Jesus.

God planted a vineyard for himself and committed its cultivation to certain tenants (the Jews). Not only did they neglect their task, but they maltreated and killed the succession of servants (the prophets of Israel—Micaiah, Jeremiah, Zechariah, etc., ending with the Baptist) whom he sent to them. At length God made his last appeal: he sent to them his only Son, hoping that they would 'respect' him. But him, too, they resolved to kill. What alternative was left to God but to end his contract (or covenant) with them, and transfer the privilege of the vineyard to others?

In other words, the allegory describes the climax of God's dealings with his people, makes clear the unique place which Jesus knew himself to hold in the purposes of God, and hints darkly at the awful judgment on the Jews to follow on their rejection of God's last appeal. Stephen's speech in Acts 7 is really a sermon on this parable.

1. A certain man planted a vineyard
Cf. Isa. 5. 1-7 and especially the last verse: 'For the vineyard of the Lord of hosts is the house of Israel.' THE WINEFAT. The winepress in which the grapes were trodden out. TOWER. For a watchman to guard the fruit.

2.
It was customary in those days for a tenant farmer to pay his rent in a part of the produce.

6. One son, his well-beloved
Agapetos may here mean (as Turner argues) 'only'.

7. This is the heir
What a tremendous claim is made in one word! Jesus is the Son to whom the Father says continually, 'Son, thou art ever with me, and all that I have is thine'. The same tremendous claim emerges in 'the great Doxology' (Matt. 11. 27; Luke 10. 22).

9. He will come and destroy
A clear prediction of the ruin that came upon Jerusalem in A.D. 70, with a veiled prophecy of the new Israel, i.e. the Christian Church.

10 f.
Ps. 118. 22 f. A tradition told that when Solomon's Temple was building, a stone was found without seeming purpose and was thrown away. Later, when the chief corner-stone was missing, the rejected stone was found to fit this vital place. In the Psalm the corner-stone was Israel, despised by the nations, but destined to supremacy. So Jesus, despised and rejected, will yet become the corner-stone of salvation.

THE QUESTION ABOUT TRIBUTE MONEY

12. 13-17 (Matt. 22. 15-22; Luke 20. 20-26)

As Judea was directly under Roman rule, every Jew living there had to pay the Roman tribute. This tax, which went into the emperor's privy purse, had to be paid in silver *denarii* (a denarius was worth about ninepence) which bore the name and effigy of the emperor. To pay or not to pay was the question of questions; and if the Pharisees were on the whole for paying, their extremer representatives, the Zealots, were most emphatically not. 'No tribute to the Romans!' was their rallying-cry.

The deputation of Pharisees and Herodians, after opening with a transparent piece of flattery ('You are a straight-forward man who speaks God's truth without fear or favour'), put the question to Jesus. They obviously hoped to impale him on the horns of a dilemma. If he answered 'No', they could delate him to the Romans as a seditionary. If he answered 'Yes', he would cut a sorry figure as Messiah in the eyes of the common people.

Jesus cleverly evaded the dilemma in his answer. So long as God's rights were safeguarded (he said) there was no need to question the rights of Caesar. Civil obedience, attested by the payment of the tax, no more contradicted than it abolished the obedience due to God. (It would, of course, be utterly wrong to suppose that Jesus set the debt to Caesar on the same level with a man's duty to God.)

This was an *ad hoc* answer, not a fixed and permanent rule for every situation. Circumstances alter cases. In the present case there was much to be said for the Roman government; to its subject peoples it brought, on the whole, peace and even-handed justice. On the other hand, as we know, there arise situations in history where it becomes impossible to render unto Caesar the things that are Caesar's without compromising one's higher allegiance to God. Then, though it must almost certainly mean suffering, the Christian's duty is to obey God rather than man.

17. The things that are God's

'Give back to God that which has the image and superscription of God—the soul' (Erasmus).

DO THE DEAD RISE?

12. 18-27 (Matt. 22. 23-33; Luke 20. 27-40)

The Sadducees (the priestly aristocrats who controlled the Temple) were in theology conservatives, and rejected as new-fangled nonsense the doctrine of the Resurrection, which had become popular in the last 150 years. They clung to the older view that all God's judgments were accomplished in this world, and that it was vain to call in another to redress the injustices of this one. Some of their number now put to Jesus what was probably a stock poser in their controversies with the Pharisees.

To understand it, we must remember the Jewish law of levirate marriage, which is succinctly stated in Deut. 25. 5. This laid it down that if a man died without issue, his brother must marry his widow; a law, no doubt, designed to secure the continuance of the family line. The Sadducees select an extreme case: a woman who had seven brothers as successive husbands. All seven married the same wife. All died child-less. 'Now,' said the Sadducees, 'suppose there be such a thing as a future life, whose wife will she be in heaven? If the wife of one, of which one? If of all seven, what about monogamy?'

Jesus' reply is first of all to tax them with twofold ignorance: (a) of the scriptures, i.e. the Old Testament, where (as he will show) a future life is implied; and (b) of the power of God to create new orders of existence. He points out that conditions in the next world are very different from those in this; marriage as we know it does not exist, and all life resembles that of the angels—is one of perfect communion with God. Then he turns to rebut the Sadducees' denial of a future life, and chooses a passage from the Pentateuch (Ex. 3. 6)—the only section of the Old Testament accepted as canonical by the Sadducees—which implies a future life. 'Have you not read in the book of Moses . . . how God said to him, I am the God of Abraham and of Isaac and of Jacob. He is not the God of the dead, but of the living.'

God called these men his friends (says Jesus) and God does not leave his friends in the dust. It is on the goodness of God and on the reality of the religious life that this argument—the one great religious argument for immortality—rests. Put in brief and Christian form it runs: When God loves once, he loves for ever. '*Quod Deo non perit, sibi non perit*,' said Augustine. In essence it is the same argument with which Paul closes the eighth chapter of the *Romans*: 'I am persuaded that neither death nor life . . . shall be able to separate us from the love of God which is in Christ Jesus our Lord.'

25. As the angels

The life to come is higher than this present existence; the *spiritual* body, as Paul said, is to be different from the *natural* body (1 Cor. 15. 40-56).

26. In the bush

That is, in the passage about the (burning) bush, viz. Ex. 3. 2 ff.

WHICH IS THE CHIEF COMMANDMENT?
12. 28-34 (Matt. 22. 34-40; cf. Luke 10. 25 ff.)

This, the last question, seems to have been asked in a friendly spirit by a scribe who may have admired the masterly way in which Jesus had 'muzzled the Pharisees'. When we recall that the Rabbis counted no less than 613 commandments in the Law, the scribe's question was a reasonable one: 'Which is the first (most important) commandment?' Our Lord answers with two quotations from the Old Testament (Deut. 6. 4 f. and Lev. 19. 18) 'so stated as (1) to put in the forefront the supreme contribution of Judaism to the history of religion in the world, faith in one only God, and (2) to interpret the whole duty of man to the one God and to his fellow men in terms of the single verb "to love".'[1]

[1] Turner, *op. cit.*, p. 60.

In days gone by there was a tendency to emphasise commandment 1 to the exclusion of commandment 2. Nowadays the pendulum has swung quite the other way. Our Lord, however, puts 1 first while insisting that 1 cannot properly exist without 2; and many a man has found his way to 1 by way of 2.

29 f. The *Shema*, or Creed, which every pious Jew repeated daily and which this scribe no doubt carried in his phylactery. WITH ALL THY HEART, etc., means simply 'with all your faculties'.

31. Lev. 19. 18. Jesus culls this flower from a mass of ritual rubbish. For the Old Testament NEIGHBOUR means 'fellow Israelite'; for Jesus, as the Parable of the Good Samaritan shows (in Luke's account of this incident), it meant 'anyone in need of your help and love'.

33. Cf. Hos. 6. 6 quoted elsewhere by Jesus.

34. Thou art not far from the Kingdom of God
'You come near possessing the qualifications needed for entry into the Kingdom of God' (Rawlinson).

WHO IS THE MESSIAH?

12. 35-37 (Matt. 22. 41-46; Luke 20. 41-44)

Jesus now takes up the questioning. 'In what sense,' he asks, 'do you theologians say that the Messiah is the Son of David? Consider Psalm 110. 1, which everyone assumes to refer to the Messiah. There David (Jesus assumes the traditional authorship of the Psalms) expressly calls the Messiah his "lord". How then do you reconcile these two ideas of sonship and lordship?'

Some interpret Jesus' question as a disclaimer of Davidic descent. But surely the point is that the Messiah is an incomparably greater person than any mere scion of David's line. Jesus knew the answer to his question, though he did not give it. As David's descendant, he was to that extent subordinate to him; but as the Son of God he was his 'Lord'.

35. For CHRIST read 'the Messiah'. Otherwise an English reader misses the point.

BEWARE OF THE SCRIBES

12. 38-40 (Matt. 23. 1, 6, 7; Luke 11. 43; 20. 46 f.)

N.B.—Jesus' indictment of the scribes is to be found at greater length in Luke 11. 37-52 (Q) and Matt. 23. 1-39, which is mostly from M, Matthew's special source.

Jesus could praise a discerning scribe, as we have just seen, but the class as a whole exhibited certain sins which evoked his outspoken condemnation. One was their love of religious uniform ('ecclesiastical millinery') and public deference ('the raised hats of the laity'); a failing not yet wholly extinct in the clerical class. More serious was the sin condemned in v. 40. The scribes made material profit out of their spiritual influence, and that, too, at the expense of widows. Since Josephus speaks of the 'great influence' which certain Pharisees had over women, and the Talmud of 'the plague of the Pharisees' who advise orphans to deprive the widow of her maintenance, we know that Jesus had good grounds for his criticism. But are we to-day in any better case? 'He does not spare us, the scribes of to-day' comments Lowrie. 'Not me at least, for I go about sometimes in long robes, I like obsequious salutations, a chief seat in the synagogue, and a place of honour at banquets. Nor does he spare the pious laity, as we shall see in the next paragraph.'[1]

40. For DAMNATION read 'judgment'. Because they have received greater privileges, they will be 'examined on a higher standard' by God.

THE WIDOW'S MITES

12. 41-44 (Luke 21. 1-4)

The Treasury, situated in the Court of the Women, held thirteen trumpet-shaped boxes for donations. Contributors had to declare the amount of their offerings. What happened

[1] Lowrie, *op. cit.*, p. 463.

was probably visible and audible to Jesus through the open door of the Treasury.

Christ's point is perfectly clear. God measures our charity not by its amount, but by our means and by the spirit in which we give. In his sight the greatest gift is that which costs the giver most. One would like to think that the lesson of the Widow's Mites had engraved itself on the universal Christian conscience; but 'subscriptions lists are still dangerous things', and we tend to pay more attention to the 'fivers' of the rich than to the shillings of the really poor. Having only two mites, the widow could easily have given but one; and, by our standards, this would have been a handsome contribution.

42. Two mites (*lepta*) which make a farthing (*kodrantēs*)

The *lepton*, which was the smallest Jewish coin, was made of copper. Mark explains that two *lepta* amounted to a *buadrans* (one-quarter of an *as*). Render: 'Two copper coins which make a penny.'

XIII

THE APOCALYPTIC DISCOURSE

XIII

(MATT. 24.; LUKE 21. 5-36)

MARK 13 is the biggest problem in the Gospel. It will conduce to clearness if we first discuss it as a whole and then add notes on particular verses.

Let us begin by summarising the chapter. In the first two verses Jesus predicts the destruction of the Temple. Four disciples then ask him privately when this will happen, and in answer they are given a long discourse which, instead of developing the prophecy, maps out in apocalyptic detail the events which will lead up to the end of the world. What we get is a drama in three acts.

Act 1 describes the 'throes' or omens: a period of wars and natural calamities which will bring persecution for the disciples (5-13).

Act 2 describes the great tribulation which will be inaugurated by an outrage to the Temple. This time will come suddenly upon Judea, will bring intense suffering, but will be shortened for the sake of the elect. This stage, like the first, will witness the appearance of pseudo-Christs and deceivers (14-23).

Act 3 describes the *dénouement* or Parousia. After a cosmic catastrophe the Son of Man will appear and rescue his elect (24-27).

The remaining verses, by means of the parables of the

Fig Tree and the Absent Householder, enforce the duty of watchfulness, teaching that the end is near but its precise hour unknown (28-37).

That this discourse is composite is beyond all doubt (e.g. 15 f. is found in Luke 17. 31, Q). Much more important is the question, Is it a genuine discourse of Jesus?

Its authenticity has been challenged on the following grounds:

1. It is the only lengthy discourse in Mark.
2. It follows the pattern of a conventional Jewish apocalypse, and draws much of its language from Daniel.
3. It seems to reflect in places the life of the Church and events in the world between, say, A.D. 40 and 65.
4. Its doctrine does not square with Jesus' teaching elsewhere (e.g. Q does not teach that Jesus will return in visible glory in the lifetime of the first generation; nor does Jesus elsewhere map out the future in this crude apocalyptic fashion).

Modern scholarship therefore believes that this chapter is a Jewish Christian apocalypse containing some genuine sayings of Jesus. The writer of this apocalypse was probably a Jewish Christian, writing perhaps about A.D. 65[1] in order to reassure Christians in their time of trouble that the Lord himself had foreseen the delays in his Second Coming.

The original apocalypse perhaps consisted of vv. 5-8, 14-20, and 24-27, which make up a compact little apocalypse of the conventional Jewish sort. That this is not wholly speculative is proven by the parenthesis in v. 14 ('Let the reader understand'), which seems to imply a *written* document.

Our final question, How much of Mark 13 goes back to Jesus? We may answer in the words of H. G. Wood:

> The prediction of Jerusalem's fall, the anticipation of disaster and tribulation for his own people, the warning against anxiety whether in the presence of war or persecu-

[1] There are no clear references to events after A.D. 65—such as the invasion of Judea and the sack of Jerusalem and its Temple.

tion, the exhortation to watchfulness, clearly come from Jesus himself.'[1]

In other words, we may accept as genuine those sayings in Mark 13 which we can parallel in Jesus' teaching elsewhere: viz. vv. 1-2, 9-11, 15 f., 28-37 (see the notes).

Is, then, Mark 13 without value for the Christian? No; its main message is still relevant for the Church. It is a message for a crisis, and its purport is that the sufferings and tribulations which Christians pass through are not outside the purpose of God. The agelong conflict between good and evil will not go on for ever. In Paul's words, Christ 'must reign' and in the end the faith and perseverance of the saints must be rewarded and God be all in all.

NOTES

1-2. Herod's Temple, begun in 20 B.C., was rightly accounted one of the wonders of the world. Its magnificent masonry evokes the awed admiration of the disciples: 'Just look! What huge stones! What huge buildings!' Solemnly Jesus tells them that its doom is writ—a prophecy which came true in A.D. 70 (cf. Luke 13. 35, Q).

5-13. The beginning of the 'throes'

Wars, earthquakes, and famines were regular features in Jewish apocalypse; but we may note that there was a famine in Judea in A.D. 46 (Acts 11. 28), and that there were severe earthquakes in Pompeii and Laodicea in A.D. 61-2. With vv. 9-11 compare Luke 12. 11 f. Paul's own life well illustrates these verses; 13b is very like 2 Esdras 6. 25: 'Whosoever shall have survived all these things . . . shall be saved.'

14-23. The Great Tribulation

Verse 14 is based on Dan. 11. 31, which refers to the pollution of the Temple by Antiochus Epiphanes; but the reference here is to the Roman power and perhaps to the unsuccessful attempt of the mad Emperor Caligula in A.D. 40 to repeat the outrage of Antiochus. Vv. 15-16 are paralleled in Luke 17. 31 (Q), i.e. are a genuine utterance of

[1] H. G. Wood in Peake's *Commentary*, p. 696.

Jesus which probably predicted the panic flight of the
Judeans before the quick-marching Roman armies advancing on Jerusalem. It has been pointed out that v. 18 must
refer to the sack of Jerusalem, not the end of the world; for,
in a time of cosmic cataclysm, it would make no difference
whether it was summer or winter; v. 19 is from Dan. 12. 1,
as v. 20 recalls Dan. 12. 7; vv. 21-22 repeat 5-6, and add
a prophecy of wonder-working impostors.

24-27. The Parousia

The *dénouement* is described in language from the Old Testament; v. 24=Isa. 13. 10; v. 25=Isa. 34. 4 (LXX); v. 26=
Dan. 7. 13 f., and v. 27 suggests Zech. 2. 6 with a phrase
from Deut. 30. 4. This patchwork of O.T. testimonies (partly
in the language of the LXX) can hardly be the teaching of
Jesus.

28-37. Exhortation to watchfulness

Verse 28, the little parable of the Fig Tree, may be a saying
of Jesus. It recalls the 'Weather Signs' saying in Luke 12.
54-56. On Jesus' lips it must have been a warning to watchfulness in face of the crisis created by his ministry and
destined to issue in the destruction of Jerusalem, v. 30. We
recall that elsewhere Jesus forecast the ruin of Jerusalem
and the Jewish people within the lifetime of the existing
generation (see Luke 11. 49-51, Q); v. 32 must be a genuine
saying. No one in the early Church would have invented it.
Note the absolute use of the title SON. The little Parable of
the Absent Householder in vv. 34-36 recalls the 'Waiting
Servants' of Luke 12. 35-40 (Q). In this context the parable
refers to the Second Advent. Spoken by our Lord on the
eve of his passion, it might well refer to the short interval
before his return from the grave and vindication by God.

XIV

THE CONSPIRACY

XIV. 1-2

(MATT. 26. 1-5; LUKE 22. 1-2)

WE are now at Wednesday of Holy Week. Since the Crucifixion happened on a Friday (Mark 15. 42) and the Last Supper the night before (Thursday), the meal in Simon's house presumably took place on Wednesday evening and the conspiracy on Wednesday afternoon.

The chief priests and scribes now resolved to make a private arrest of Jesus. An open arrest was deemed inadvisable, because Jesus had many sympathisers, and a public seizure might provoke a tumult.

THE ANOINTING AT BETHANY

14. 3-9 (Matt. 26. 6-13; cf. John 12. 1-8)

(Luke omits this narrative because he had already narrated an anointing in Galilee (see Luke 7. 36-50). John locates the event 'six days before the Passover' in the home of Lazarus and his two sisters. Mary anoints Jesus' feet and wipes them with her hair. Judas makes the cavil about the waste, and Jesus says: 'Suffer her to keep it against the day of my burial.')

The story is familiar. While Jesus is reclining at supper in the house of Simon the Leper, a woman breaks a flask of very precious ointment and pours it over his head. There is

angry comment on her action. 'This might have been sold
and the proceeds given to the poor.' But Jesus, to the disciples' surprise, pronounces it 'a beautiful deed' and pro-
phesies that it will go as far in the world as the Gospel. The
woman has seized a unique opportunity; their chance of
serving Christ in the poor would continue—and is likely to
continue.

What was there in the woman's act to evoke Christ's
praise? That it was a courageous act is obvious. That it was
a costly act we are expressly told. But surely it was the
insight of the act that moved Christ to such splendid praise.
What was that insight? If we bear two things in mind—first,
that she *broke* the flask, and, second, that it was an anointing
—we shall get near its secret. For in anointing the dead it
was customary to break the flask before laying it in the
coffin, and the very name Messiah means 'Anointed One'.
In other words, the woman had penetrated into the secret
of the Suffering and Dying Messiah. Her act said more
plainly than words to Christ 'I know that you are the Messiah, and I know also that a cross awaits you'. Her woman's
intuition had brought her into spiritual places where even
the Twelve were strangers.

3. Simon the leper

He must have been a cured leper, or there would scarcely
have been a banquet in his house. One wonders if Jesus had
cured him. AN ALABASTER BOX OF OINTMENT. Alabastron was
a place in Egypt where they quarried a fine marble used for
making flasks. SPIKENARD. The Greek is *pistic nard*. No one
knows for certain what *pistic* means. It may mean 'potable'
(from *pino*, I drink). It may mean made of the *pistachio nut*,
whose resin was often mixed with oil of nard. Most probably
'pistic' is from the same root as *pistis* and means 'pure' or
'genuine'.

THE BETRAYAL

14. 10-11 (Matt. 26. 14-16; Luke 22. 3-6)

Why did Judas betray Jesus, and what did he disclose to
the chief priests? What Judas disclosed, says Schweitzer, was

the Messiahship of Jesus. If that were so, why was not Judas called as the star witness at the trial? Moreover, by this time the Messianic secret must have been a pretty open one. Therefore the explanation implied in the text is much to be preferred: what Judas divulged was when and where Jesus might be *conveniently* arrested. For 'Judas . . . knew the place' (John 18. 2).

But why did Judas betray Jesus? Of many guesses the best known is perhaps that of De Quincey. Judas, he says, wished to force Jesus into a situation where he would be compelled to display his divine power, but with no idea that Jesus would allow himself to be killed. This is sheer speculation: there is not a tittle of evidence to support it. It springs, no doubt, from some desire to 'whitewash' the traitor,[1] from a reluctance to believe that one whom Jesus called to be a disciple could have betrayed his Master in cold blood. Far likelier is it that Jesus' conception of his Messiahship bitterly disappointed Judas (did not even Peter boggle at it?) and that, sensing the peril in which Jesus and his disciples stood, he seized the last chance to extricate himself from it (as well as the chance of making some money) by 'turning king's evidence'.

11. Money

According to Matt. 26. 15, thirty pieces of silver.

PREPARATIONS FOR THE PASSOVER
14. 12-16 (Matt. 26. 17-19; Luke 22. 7-13)

Mark suggests that the Last Supper was a Passover meal (see 14. 12, 16), while elsewhere implying that Jesus was crucified before the Feast (see 14. 2 and 15. 42). John, however, consistently testifies that Jesus was crucified on the day of the killing of the Passover lamb (John 13. 1; 18. 28; 19. 31). Can the Last Supper have been a Passover? This is

[1] 'I refuse,' said George Eliot, speaking of this view, 'to accept a man who has the stomach for such treachery as a hero impatient for the redemption of mankind.'

an old controversy, and into the technical pros and cons we cannot go here. Suffice it to say that modern scholars, with one or two exceptions, prefer John's testimony. In that case the Last Supper was probably either (*a*) a hurried anticipation of the Passover (Jesus knowing that he would be dead before the Feast), or (*b*) Passover *Kiddush* ('sanctification'), i.e. a social-religious meal, held by groups of pious Jews, in order to prepare for the Passover. Whichever it was, clearly there must have been much of the Passover atmosphere about the meal.

We need not find any miraculous elements in Jesus' arrangements for the Last Supper. Obviously he had made a previous agreement with some staunch friend for the use of 'a big upper room ready furnished' (15). The man bearing the water-pot (in the East these are mostly carried by women) looks like a pre-arranged signal between Jesus and the owner of the house. It is no more than a guess, but, as guesses go, a probable one that the house was that belonging to the mother of John Mark (cf. Acts 12. 12).

12. The first day of unleavened bread when they killed the Passover

A somewhat loose expression, meaning on the day the sunset of which was the beginning of the Feast.

13. Two of his disciples

Peter and John (Luke 22. 8).

14. The guestchamber

For THE read, with the R.V., 'my'. The 'my' is full of meaning, for Jesus was to be Host at the banquet, the disciples his guests.

16. They made ready the Passover

If it was a proper Passover, the requisites were the lamb, unleavened bread, bitter herbs, a sauce called *charoseth*, and wine.

THE ANNOUNCEMENT OF THE TRAITOR

14. 17-21 (Matt. 26. 20-25; Luke 22. 14, 21-23)

At the Last Supper Jesus and the Twelve did not sit, but reclined. We are to picture not so much one table as three, arranged thus ▭, with the fourth side left open. Couches almost level with the tables were placed outside. On these the guests reclined, each on his left arm, with his feet extended outward. (So we can understand how 'the beloved disciple' could 'lie on Jesus' breast'. He would be next to Jesus, with his back towards him, so that by bending back his head he could speak to him. Perhaps Judas was next to Jesus on the other side.)

In Mark Jesus simply says that the traitor is in the room with them. It is Matthew and John who record that Jesus singled him out. This must have been done secretly. Nor does Mark tell us when Judas left the room. For this we are indebted to John 13. 30: 'He then having received the sop went out straightway: and it was night.'

20. That dippeth with me in the dish
The DISH is the sauce dish in which all dipped their morsels.

21. As it is written of him
Beyond reasonable doubt Jesus is referring to Isa. 53. His words mean: 'The Son of Man travels the road marked out for the Suffering Servant of the Lord, but alas for that man through whose agency he is being delivered up!' The 'delivering-up' is that predicted for the Servant: 'And he bore the sins of many and was delivered up because of their iniquities' (Isa. 53. 12, LXX).

THE LAST SUPPER

14. 22-25 (Matt. 26. 26-29; Luke 22. 15-20; 1 Cor. 11. 23-25)

There are parallel accounts of the Last Supper in Matthew (who closely follows Mark) and in Luke (where we are not sure of the true text); but the most interesting parallel is Paul's account of the Last Supper in 1 Cor. 11. 23-25.

When we compare this with Mark, we note the following differences:

1. Paul alone records Christ's command to repeat the rite. (No doubt by Mark's time this was so axiomatic that he does not insert the command.)
2. Paul's version of the word over the Loaf is: 'This is my body which is for you' (R.V. Mark has 'This is my body').
3. Paul's version of the word over the Cup is: 'This cup is the new Covenant in my blood' (R.V. Mark has 'This is my blood of the covenant which is shed for many').

Despite these variations the two accounts agree on the essentials. At the Last Supper, Jesus, after saying a grace over the loaf, broke it and gave it to the disciples with the word: 'This is my body.' Then he gave them the cup with the ruddy wine gleaming in it, saying: 'This [cup] is the [new] covenant in my blood.' Clearly he spoke of a covenant —a new order of relations between God and man—to be established by his blood, i.e. by his life freely surrendered to God.

In order to understand what he said and did,[1] let us recall three things:

(a) Jesus had likened the Kingdom of God to a supper or banquet (see the Parable of the Great Feast, Luke 14. 15-24, Q).
(b) The Passover commemorated the redemptive act of God by which he had marked out Israel as his special People. But Jesus had declared that the Jews by rejecting their Messiah were no longer God's People, and had foretold the creation of a new Israel (see Mark 12. 9 and Luke 13. 34 f., Q).
(c) He had affirmed that he was giving his life to redeem 'the many' (Mark 10. 45; cf. Mark 14. 24), and had described his passion as a 'cup' to be drunk (Mark 10. 38; 14. 36).

[1] This interpretation owes much to C. H. Dodd. See *A Companion to the Bible* (Ed. T W. Manson), pp. 386 f.

All three ideas—the Kingdom as a banquet, the new People of God, his death as a cup to be drunk—contribute to our understanding of the Last Supper.

In setting apart the bread and the wine, Jesus was offering the disciples a pledge of life in the Kingdom.

In describing the broken loaf as his body and the out-poured wine as his blood, he was effecting, in symbol, that sacrifice he was soon to accomplish in fact. And by asking the disciples to partake he was giving them a share in the virtue of that sacrifice—'a share in the power of the broken Christ' (Otto).

There is a splendid symbolism here, but something more. The act is an effective sign, a sacrament, for all who accept it in faith. When the disciples rose from the supper table they rose as men redeemed by the sacrifice of their Lord, as men to whom the Kingdom of God was given. 'The Twelve sat that night,' says Hort truly, 'as representatives of the Church at large.'[1]

But the disciples were still sinful men? Of course they were. This is the last and finest illustration of one of Jesus' supreme truths—that the grace of God is given to undeserving men. ('Tak' it, woman,' said 'Rabbi' Duncan centuries later to a woman who shrank from receiving the Communion chalice, 'tak' it. It's for sinners.')

24. Testament
Better 'covenant'. The two chief Old Testament passages which supply the background for this saying are Ex. 24. 4-8 (the Covenant at Sinai) and Jer. 31. 31-34 (Jeremiah's prophecy of the new Covenant).

25. The word NEW (*kainos*) means new in quality, not in time. Christ is thinking of the new world beyond this one —the supernal world—where God's Kingdom does not come, but is eternally present. He will not taste wine again until he tastes it in the presence of God.

ON THE WAY TO GETHSEMANE
14. 26-31 (Matt. 26. 30-35; Luke 22. 39)

With the singing of psalms the little company now leave

[1] F. J. A. Hort, *The Christian Ecclesia*, p. 30.

the Upper Room and pass out into the night. Their route lies through the City Gate, down the steep bank of the Kidron, and across the winter torrent to the Mount of Olives. As they go, Jesus sadly predicts their desertion of him, quoting Zech. 13. 7 (note the pastoral image). Peter strongly demurs. He will go, if need be alone, to death with Jesus. 'Before the night is out,' replies Jesus, 'you will deny me three times.'

26. A hymn

The Greek (*hymnēsantes*) need not mean only one hymn, or rather psalm. If the meal was a Passover, or a hurried anticipation of it, their praise would consist of the second half of the Hallel Psalms (115-118), the 'Songs of Praise' usually sung at the great festivals.

28. I will go before you into Galilee

Jesus predicts his resurrection, using a pastoral verb: 'I will lead you like a shepherd.' Though its end is lost, Mark's Gospel was clearly leading up to an appearance of the Risen Lord in Galilee (see John 21).

30. Before the cock crow twice

Classical writers mention the second cock-crow (*gallicinium*) as a note of time. We are to think not of the cry of a bird, but of a trumpet note.

THE AGONY

14. 32-42 (Matt 26. 36-46; Luke 22. 40-46)

The story of the Agony, told by Mark in all its stark simplicity, is as moving as anything in human literature.

As they near the olive grove called Gethsemane our Lord feels the intense need of prayer at this supreme hour of spiritual crisis. Eight of his disciples he leaves on the fringe of the grove. The other three—Peter, James, and John—who had seen his glory on the Mount of Transfiguration, he now takes with him to share his vigil and witness his agony. A deadly desolation descends on his spirit and he tells them something of it in words taken from Ps. 42. 6. Then advancing a few paces (yet not so far that they could not hear the

main drift of his words) he supplicates his Father for the
removal of the cup. It is the old temptation—Messiahship
without a cross, salvation without atonement—that meets
him here for the last time and with redoubled force. But he
has no sooner prayed for the cup's removal than he quietly
resigns himself to the Father's sovereign will. Twice he re-
turns to find the disciples sleeping. On the third occasion
the stillness of the grove is broken by the sound of the
approaching posse.

On the scene as a whole two comments from very different
writers are permissible. The first is from the Jew, Montefiore:

> The lesson of Gethsemane speaks to us all. If we learn
> from the lives of heroes, we, too, have something here to
> learn. How much strength has the recollection of the
> prayer in Gethsemane given to endless human souls.'[1]

The other is from the Unitarian, James Martineau:

> A voice upon the midnight air
>   Where Kedron's moonlit waters stray
> Weeps forth, in agony of prayer,
>   'O Father, take this cup away!'
>
> Ah, thou, who sorrowest unto death,
>   We conquer in thy mortal fray;
> And earth for all her children saith,
>   'O God, take not this cup away!'[2]

36. This cup

As in 10. 38, it is the cup of affliction, the cup our sins had
mingled, which he as the Suffering Servant of the Lord must
drink to the dregs if the many are to be redeemed. Note that
Mark preserves the very Aramaic word ABBA which Jesus
used, but he adds the word 'Father' (*Pater*) for the benefit
of his Gentile readers (cf. Rom. 8. 15 and Gal. 4. 6). Jesus
could say 'Abba, thy will be done' to the God who was
delivering him up to a cross. Could we?

[1] Montefiore, *The Synoptic Gospels*, p. 344.
[2] Martineau in *Songs of Praise*, No. 124.

38. Lest ye enter into temptation

Recalls the petition in the Lord's Prayer. The disciples' temptation was to irremediable apostasy, to 'hatred of this man who had so wooed them away from this world that never again would they be contented with it'.

41. It is enough

The single Greek word (*apechei*) can hardly have this meaning. Its normal meaning is 'be distant'. Therefore it is best to read here (with some MSS.): *apechei to telos* ('the end is far away'), and to regard SLEEP ON NOW, etc., as a question: 'Are you still sleeping and taking your rest?' says Jesus. 'The end is far away? The hour is come!' RISE, LET US GO. To meet the approaching party. An advance, not a retreat.

THE ARREST
14. 43-52 (Matt. 26. 47-56; Luke 22. 47-53, cf. John 18. 2-11)

The Sanhedrin, who possessed the power of arrest in certain cases, had assembled a rudely armed band with the traitor as guide. The kiss with which the pupil normally saluted his Rabbi was the concerted signal. Jesus himself offered no resistance, but one of his followers (whom John names as Peter) drew his sword and cut off the ear of the High Priest's servant (whose name, John says, was Malchus). The sense of our Lord's question is, 'Do you think me a common bandit? Why did you not seize your chance while I was teaching in the Temple? But the scriptures (i.e. Isa. 53) must be fulfilled.' Then the disciples made their escape in the darkness. Having secured the leader, the arresting party were content to let the rest go.

51 f. Neither Matthew nor Luke thought it worthwhile to copy these verses from Mark. They seemed so trivial and pointless. Why did Mark insert them? There is only one good explanation. They refer to himself. They are his modest way of saying, 'I was there'. If the Upper Room was in his mother's house, we may surmise that some of the arresting party had called there first, and that Mark, sensing the situation, had hurried out to warn Jesus.

THE TRIAL BEFORE CAIAPHAS
14. 53-65 (Matt. 26. 57-68; Luke 22. 54 f., 63-71)

The Trial of our Lord falls into two parts: (1) ecclesiastical, and (2) civil. Basing ourselves on Mark's record, but using the evidence of the other evangelists, we may set forth the sequence of events as follows:

A. *Ecclesiastical Trial:* on the charge of blasphemy
   (1) Jesus is tried by the Sanhedrin under Caiaphas and is found guilty. But these midnight proceedings are irregular, because formal meetings of the Council were only legal between sunrise and sunset. Therefore
   (2) At dawn a formal meeting of the Council confirms the informal verdict. The Sanhedrin, however, had no power to execute a capital sentence. On the other hand the Roman Governor would not listen to a charge of blasphemy. So there follows:

B. *The Civil Trial:* on the charge of treason
   (1) Before Pilate.
   (2) Pilate tries to remit the case to Herod (Luke 23. 7-12).
   (3) Final trial before Pilate, who sentences Jesus to crucifixion.

With this summary we may now return to Mark's narrative. At midnight an informal gathering of the Sanhedrin under Caiaphas, the reigning High Priest, was hastily convened. Apparently it took some time to reach a verdict. There were accusations in plenty, but the merciful provision of Deut. 19. 15 laid it down that the unsupported evidence of a single witness should not stand. Then somebody remembered a saying of Jesus about 'destroying the Temple' (cf. Mark 13. 2), but even on this point they could not get the witnesses to tell the same consistent story. Finally Caiaphas took the matter into his own hands. 'Are you the Messiah, the Son of the Blessed (God)?' he asked. If, in face of the Temple charge, our Lord had been silent, in face of this one he makes instant answer 'I am', passing at once to avow that he was destined to triumph and obtain the highest place that heaven affords. This answer Caiaphas at once pro-

nounces to be blasphemy, of which the penalty was death
(Lev. 24. 16). One and all declare him to be worthy of the
extreme penalty—a penalty which they could not themselves
inflict. Before Jesus leaves the Sanhedrin's palace some of
its members insult him, and the guards join in.

58. I will destroy this temple

Jesus had undoubtedly said something to this effect (cf.
Mark 15. 29; John 2. 19; Acts 6. 14). But probably his saying
was a prophecy that, though the Temple was doomed, he
would raise a new spiritual shrine for the worship of the true
People of God.

61. But he held his peace

So it was written of the Servant of the Lord that 'he opened
not his mouth' (Isa. 53. 7).

62. Ye shall see the Son of Man, etc.

Jesus' words are taken from Dan. 7. 13, with a phrase ('sitting at the right hand of Power', i.e. God) from Ps. 110. 1.
It is very important to note that they predict *not a descent,
but an ascent*. Observe the context in Daniel. There the verse
which begins 'There came with the clouds of heaven one
like unto a son of man' ends 'and he came even to the
Ancient of days, and they brought him near before him'.
In Daniel the Son of man's destination is the immediate
presence of God. Likewise, the words on our Lord's lips,
so far from being a prophecy of the Second Coming (as is
generally assumed), are a prediction that he will be exalted
to the presence of God. In short, Jesus' reply is an im-
passioned assertion that, despite the apparent ruin of his
cause, he will yet be gloriously vindicated by God. 'I shall
be received by God to the supreme place of honour,' he says
in effect, 'and this my exaltation you shall know.'

63. Then the high priest rent his clothes

Like the putting on of the black cap, this was a formal act
to be gone through when a man was convicted of blasphemy.
'The rent had come to be of specified length, and to apply
to specified clothes, those in fact which could be most easily
mended '

64. They all condemned him

They could not actually pass sentence of death. Yet with Jesus' confession of Messiahship they now had something which could easily be converted into a *political* charge of claiming to be 'King of the Jews'. And if the Roman Pilate could not be expected to do much about a Messianic claim, he could not ignore a charge of conspiracy against Caesar.

65. Prophesy

Either (as Matthew and Luke interpret) 'Prophesy who smote thee', i.e. a grim game of Blind Man's Buff, or 'Let us hear some more of your prophecies'.

PETER'S DENIAL
14. 66-72 (Matt. 26. 69-75; Luke 22. 56-62)

The story of the denial, which must surely go back to Peter himself, is full of salutary rebuke for our own Christian living.

Verse 54 found Peter 'right inside the High Priest's Court' (John 18. 15 f. tells us how he got there) sitting by the fire with the servants. Since he was 'down below' in the court (66), the Sanhedrin were presumably sitting upstairs. After the maidservant's first challenge he moved into the *proaulion* or 'outer court' (A.V. 'porch'), where it would be colder, but —lacking the firelight—also safer. The stammering redundancy of Peter's first denial vividly expresses his embarrassment: 'I neither know nor understand what you mean.' There followed a second challenge and a second denial. Then the bystanders, no doubt noting his dialect (cf. Matt. 26. 73, 'Thy speech bewrayeth thee'; the Galileans spoke with a rough burr), repeated the challenge, and Peter's self-respect went by the board. Scarcely had he denied his Master with oaths when the cock crew, touching a chord of memory, and Peter dissolved in bitter tears.

70. Omit the words 'and thy speech agreeth thereto.

71. He began to curse and to swear

Two different words in the Greek. The first, CURSE (*anathematizein*), means to call down an anathema on oneself if one

is lying. The second, SWEAR (*omnuein*), means to assert with
an oath. Jesus had forbidden such speech (Matt. 5. 34-37),
saying that it came from the devil. As Matthew Henry ob-
serves, 'We have reason to suspect the truth of that which
is backed with oaths and rash imprecations. None but the
devil's sayings need the devil's proofs.'

72. And when he thought thereon, he wept

The single Greek word (*epibalon*), translated WHEN HE
THOUGHT THEREON, means literally 'having applied', and we
have to understand 'his mind thereto'. Papyri usage suggests
that the sentence may mean simply 'And he set to and wept'.
It is Luke who tells us that the Lord 'looked upon Peter'
(Luke 22. 61).

XV

THE TRIAL BEFORE PILATE

XV. 1-15

(MATT. 27. 1-2, 11-26; LUKE 23. 1-25)

(The parallel accounts should be compared. Matthew, who
follows Mark, inserts the two episodes about Pilate's wife's
dream and his hand-washing. Luke, who seems to have had
special information, tells us (1) of the actual charge laid before Pilate, and (2) of the sending of Jesus to Herod.)

At dawn a formal meeting of the Sanhedrin confirmed the
decision taken at midnight. Having secured the basis for a
political charge (see Luke 23. 2, which probably summarises
it), they now took their prisoner to the palace of the Pro-
curator, who alone had power to pass the death sentence
they desired. Pilate, whom Josephus calls 'inflexible, merci-
less and obstinate', here appears in a slightly better light.
He seems to have regarded Jesus as technically guilty but
politically harmless. There has been some dispute about the
meaning of Jesus' reply to his question 'Are you the King
of the Jews?' The Greek means 'It is you who say it' (*su
legeis*). This can hardly be a direct 'Yes'. It may be a non-
committal answer. But perhaps it is best taken as a qualified
assent: 'The phrase is yours. I should not put it so, for my
Kingdom is not of this world' (cf. John 18. 36). After this

Jesus made no further answer, though his enemies redoubled their accusations.

The episode of Barabbas is interesting, historically and theologically. Evidently it was usual for the Roman Governor on a great occasion like the Feast of the Passover (when, incidentally, he moved his residence from Caesarea on the coast to Jerusalem) to show the subject people some mark of grace, like the release of a well-known political prisoner. If we have no Jewish evidence for this custom, there is pagan evidence in an Egyptian papyrus of A.D. 85 which describes the trial of a certain Phibius and says: 'You deserve to be flogged, but I will give you as a present to the people.' Barabbas (we may surmise) had been the ringleader in some anti-Roman movement which had culminated in a bloody clash. If the variant reading in Matt. 27. 17 ('Whom do you want me to release to you, Jesus Barabbas or Jesus who is called Messiah?') be accepted—and it is probable—then the insurgent bore the same name as our Lord. It is also one of the ironies of history that Barabbas probably means 'son of the father'. That the crowd preferred Barabbas to Jesus is but the supreme instance of how men so often prefer darkness to light:

> A murderer they save,
> The Prince of Life they slay.[1]

Mark hints that the priests played on the mob's love for an agitator who had given Rome trouble. Pilate, who was cynically clear-headed enough to detect the malice of the priests in the whole business, protested Jesus' innocence again; but when the popular clamour for his crucifixion was renewed, he weakly gratified their wish, and, after having Jesus scourged (a normal preliminary to execution, not a gratuitous cruelty), gave the order for his crucifixion. For Pilate, Jesus was doubtless just one more rebel against Rome, though patently an innocuous and other-worldly one. He had executed Galilean rebels before (Luke 13. 1), as he would execute them yet again before he finally lost his job. One wonders if there is any truth in Anatole France's guess that

[1] Samuel Crossman (1624-84); *Songs of Praise*, No. 127.

later Pilate completely forgot Jesus. Yet the world remembers Pilate, and remembers him because of him who 'suffered under Pontius Pilate'. So the verdicts of history are
reversed.

1. Consultation
Better 'council'.

3. But he answered nothing
Not in the best MSS. Omit.

15. Content (satisfy)
SCOURGED. The instrument was a leather whip loaded with
metal or bone.

THE MOCKING BY THE SOLDIERS
15. 16-20 (Matt. 27. 27-31; cf. John 19. 1-3)

(Luke, who omits this section, describes a mocking by
Herod's men, 23. 11.)

Jesus had been stripped for scourging. Before re-clothing
him, the soldiers indulge in a bit of grim barrack-room jest-
ing, based on the accusation brought against Jesus. He has
claimed to be a king (they argue); let us give him a taste of
kingly honours. So, procuring a soldier's red cloak (to represent the imperial purple), a circlet made from some handy
thorns (corresponding to the imperial diadem), and (as Matt.
27. 29 records) a reed to serve as sceptre, they dress him up
in pseudo-regal style and insultingly kneel down in mock
homage before him. Then, putting his clothes on him, they
lead him out to crucifixion. It is a sickening scene: the
humiliation of the Servant of the Lord is complete.

16. Praetorium
A Latin word originally meaning 'the General's tent' and
then, as here, the Governor's residence; probably in this
case Herod's palace. BAND (*speira*), literally, 'cohort'.
'Platoon' would probably be the best rendering

18. Hail, King of the Jews
A parody of 'Hail, Caesar' (*Ave, Caesar*).

19. Worshipped (*prosekunoun*)
'Prostrated themselves before him.'

THE CRUCIFIXION

15. 21-32 (Matt. 27. 32-44; Luke 23. 26-43)

(Luke supplements Mark with two sayings ('Daughters of Jerusalem' and 'Father, forgive them') and the episode of the penitent thief.)

Jesus probably set out for Golgotha carrying his own cross (or rather, the transom or cross-piece; see John 19. 17). When he sank down exhausted under it, the Roman soldiers, who would not lower themselves to such a task, 'impressed' the first Jewish passer-by to bear the load. Simon, who was entering the city as the procession left it, is called 'a Cyrenian . . . father of Alexander and Rufus'. Cyrene in North Africa (near Benghazi in Tripoli) was a Greek settlement containing many Jews. Simon was probably not (as Church tradition has sometimes assumed) an African negro, but one of the Jewish settlers coming up for the Passover. There is only one good reason why Mark names his sons; they must have been well known in the Church, and we guess that Paul names one of them when he writes in Rom. 16. 13 'Salute Rufus, the chosen in the Lord, and his mother and mine'.

Golgotha (whose Latin equivalent is Calvary) was probably a skull-shaped eminence outside the northern city wall. Before crucifixion it was usual to offer the doomed men a potion of drugged wine—an anodyne provided by some charitable women in Jerusalem. Our Lord refused it, possibly because he wished to die with his senses undulled,[1] probably because he had sworn to drink no more wine this side of eternity (Mark 14. 25). At THE THIRD HOUR (9 a.m.), probably the hour fixed by Pilate, Jesus was crucified, and the soldiers began to while away the time by dicing for his garments, which were their perquisite. On the cross, above his head, was nailed the *titulus* or superscription, a chalked board setting forth the charge on which he had been condemned: THE KING OF THE JEWS. But his was not the only cross: Jesus

[1] Dr. Johnson, being informed that only a miracle could save him, said: 'Then I will take no more physic, even my opiates; but I have prayed that I may render up my soul to God unclouded.' In this resolution he persevered.

was flanked by two brigands, probably accomplices of Barabbas, whom tradition names Dysmas and Gestas. As he hung there, some of the passers-by, the chief priests and scribes, and even the two bandits, shouted their jeers at him. HE SAVED OTHERS, HIMSELF HE CANNOT SAVE. The mocking sneer was true. He had come to save others. It had been his chief temptation to save himself, but he could not save himself and finish the work his Father had given him to do. 'Let the Christ, the King of Israel, now come down from the cross, that we may see and believe,' they said. 'The Jews,' commented General Booth memorably, 'would have believed in him if he had come down from the cross. We believe in him because he stayed up.'

22. No one knows the site of Golgotha. But Gordon's Calvary certainly answers to the description.

24. Cf. Ps. 22. 18 and John 19. 23-24 (the seamless robe).

28. Not in the R.V. The quotation, which is from Isa. 53. 12, is probably a scribe's gloss from Luke 22. 37.

THE DEATH OF JESUS
15. 33-41 (Matt. 27. 45-56; Luke 23. 44-49)

(Matthew adds the story of the earthquake and the resurrection of the Jewish saints. Luke adds the saying 'Father, into thy hands'.)

From noon till 3 p.m. a strange darkness, probably due (as the Roman Catholic scholar Lagrange suggests) to 'a black sirocco', covered the land. At 3 p.m. Jesus uttered the cry of dereliction: 'My God, my God, why hast thou forsaken me?' The words, which come from the first verse of Ps. 22 ('The Psalm of the Righteous Sufferer'), have been construed by some as 'a declaration of faith', because later in the Psalm the speaker reaffirms his trust in God. But if this were so, it is passing strange that Jesus should have chosen the least suitable verse in the Psalm. It is better to admit that the words express a real, though temporary, feeling of desolation and to explain that feeling in terms of

Jesus' preoccupation 'with the fact and burden of sin'. In other words, as Vincent Taylor phrases it, 'Jesus so closely identified himself with sinners and experienced the horror of sin to such a degree, that for a time the closeness of his communion with the Father was broken, so that his face was obscured and he seemed to be forsaken by him'.[1]

Some bystanders, hearing the cry, ironically suggested that the twice-repeated ELOI, ELOI (or, as Matthew gives it, 'Eli, eli') meant that he was invoking Elias (Elijah) to his help. Another man (one of the soldiers?), apparently in face of demurrers, offered Jesus a spongeful of vinegar, saying, 'Give me leave. Let us see whether Elijah will come to take him down'. Then suddenly, after six hours of torture, Jesus uttered a loud cry and 'surrendered his spirit'.

Mark adds that at that hour the curtain in the Temple separating the Holy of Holies from the Holy Place was torn from top to bottom—a fact which later writers found pregnant with spiritual truth. By his atoning death our Lord had opened up a complete and unhindered access to God (see Heb. 6. 19 f., 10. 19 f.).

Tradition names as Petronius (or Longinus) the centurion in command of the soldiers at the foot of the cross. Perhaps it was our Lord's whole demeanour during Trial and Crucifixion—so utterly unlike that of the usual criminal—which wrung from him the testimony, 'Truly this was a son of God' (cf. Luke: 'Certainly this was a righteous man'). The words, on this pagan's lips, do not represent the full Christian confession of faith; but if they mean no more than 'this was a god-like man', they are still a truly remarkable tribute from this hard-bitten Roman soldier.[2]

34. Mark gives the Aramaic, Matthew the Hebrew words of Ps. 22. 1. Probably Jesus used the Hebrew.

40. Mary the mother of James the less

In the East, to this day, a woman is often designated thus by her son's name. So Mrs. David Livingstone was called 'Ma Robert'.

[1] *Jesus and His Sacrifice*, p. 162.
[2] The Wisdom of Solomon, 2. 18: 'For if the righteous man is God's son, he will uphold him.'

41. Cf. Luke 8. 3. Were the women Mark's informants for the story of the Crucifixion?

THE BURIAL

15. 42-47 (Matt. 27. 57-61; Luke 23. 50-56)

The Friday on which Jesus died was the day of preparation for the Sabbath, which began at sunset. Only a few hours therefore remained for the task of burial. The other reason for haste was the instruction in the Law (Deut. 21. 23): 'His body shall not remain all night upon the tree, but thou shalt surely bury him the same day.' At this point Joseph of Arimathea (possibly a village north of Jerusalem) screwed up his courage and asked Pilate for the body of Jesus. His action shows high moral courage; it was not usual to ask for a criminal's body. Pilate, after assuring himself that Jesus was really dead—for crucified men often lingered in agony for days—'granted the corpse' to Joseph, who shrouded it decently and laid it in a rock tomb. Mary of Magdala and another Mary, who presumably were not known to Joseph, watched the process of entombment from a distance. The curtain seemed to have fallen on unrelieved tragedy.

43. Honourable counsellor

A member of the Sanhedrin of good social position. That he WAITED FOR THE KINGDOM OF GOD does not necessarily mean that he was a secret disciple of Jesus. It may mean only that he sympathised with the Messianic hope of the times.

46. Fine linen

Literally, 'a linen cloth'. Matthew says that the tomb belonged to Joseph, and Luke and John add that it had never been used. The purpose of the circular stone was to keep out prowling men and beasts. John adds that Joseph had the help of Nicodemus, and that the tomb was in a garden close to Calvary.

XVI

THE RESURRECTION

XVI. 1-8

(MATT. 28. 1-8; LUKE 24. 1-9)

T HE women did nothing on the Sabbath; but when it ended at sunset on Saturday they bought spices for the anointing of Jesus' body. On the first day of the week, Sunday, thenceforward to be called the Lord's Day (Rev. 1. 10), just after sunrise, Mary of Magdala with Mary the mother of James and Salome approached the tomb. They found the stone rolled away from the mouth of the tomb and, at its entrance, a young man sitting on the right side, his appearance proclaiming him a visitant from another world. 'Be not amazed,' he said. 'Are you seeking Jesus of Nazareth, who was crucified? He has risen; he is not here. See the place where they laid him. But go and tell his disciples and Peter he is going before you into Galilee (there shall you see him) as he told you.' In a terrified trance they fled from the tomb, saying not a word to any, FOR THEY WERE AFRAID . . .

5. Mark speaks of one, Luke and John of two angels: a fact which has caused difficulty to some. 'Cold discrepancy-mongers,' comments Lessing, 'do ye not see then that the evangelists do not count the angels? There were not only two angels, there were millions of them.'

6. Ye seek
Should probably be taken as a question 'Do ye seek . . .?'

7. And Peter

A special message for Peter, who had denied his Master and in his remorse might feel that Christ never wanted to see him again. The first appearance of the Risen Lord recorded by St. Paul was to *Cephas* (1 Cor. 15. 5; cf. Luke 24. 34 and John 21). Christ does not break the bruised reed. THERE SHALL YE SEE HIM. Probably a parenthesis, as in the translation given above.

8. For they were afraid (*ephobounto gar*)

With these words the authentic text of Mark comes to an abrupt end. Vv. 9-20 known as *The Longer Ending* are the work of a later hand, not of Mark. The evidence for this is threefold:

(*a*) Vv. 9-20 are not in our oldest and best MSS.

(*b*) Their style is quite unlike Mark's.

(*c*) Their contents are demonstrably a patchwork, mostly drawn from Luke and Acts.

Moreover, in some MSS. we have another ending, usually called *The Shorter Ending*, as follows:

And all that had been commanded them they briefly reported to Peter and those who were with him. And after this Jesus himself appeared to them, and from the east and as far as to the west sent forth to them the sacred and incorruptible proclamation of eternal salvation.

Why, then, does Mark's Gospel end as it does? There are three theories, which we may sum up in three words: completed; interrupted; and mutilated.

(1) The first is that Mark meant to end his Gospel just as we have it. This is incredible. Not to mention that the Greek particle *gar* ('for') is a very odd ending to a book, it is clear that Mark meant to lead up to an appearance of the Risen Lord in Galilee (cf. 14. 28).

(2) A likelier view is that Mark was interrupted before he could complete his Gospel. How he was interrupted, we can only speculate. Was it by the Neronian persecution?

(3) But the likeliest view is that the Gospel was accidentally mutilated through the end of the papyrus roll being torn off. This must have happened very early, for neither Matthew nor Luke, who used Mark in the composition of their Gospels, seem to have known the lost ending of Mark. Nobody knows what the lost ending must have contained, save that it must have recorded one or more appearances of the Risen Lord. Of these, one must have been an appearance to Peter. It is an attractive guess of Streeter's that John 21 preserves a part, if not all, of the lost ending.

Yet though the ending is lost, we have enough to show us what the sequel to the Crucifixion was. Jesus could not be 'holden of death'. What had seemed tragedy became shining victory. Out of the ruin of Calvary came the Easter Fact and the Easter Message to which the other Gospels and the rest of the New Testament documents bear irrefragable testimony. (See the concluding Essay on the Resurrection.)

NOTES ON THE LONGER ENDING

9-11 are an abridged version of John 20. 11-18 (the *Rabboni* story).

12-13 summarise Luke 24. 13-35 (the walk to Emmaus).

14-15 recall Luke 24. 36-49 and Matt. 28. 16-20.

17-18 Most of the signs here described can be paralleled in the Acts.

19   Cf. Acts 1. 9-11.

ESSAY 2—THE RESURRECTION OF JESUS CHRIST

Our earliest evidence for the Resurrection is to be found in 1 Cor. 15. 3 ff. There, Paul, writing about A.D. 55, quotes the Church tradition which he 'received' after his conversion (A.D. 33?). This tradition, which implies the empty tomb, lists five appearances of the Risen Lord besides the appearance to St. Paul himself: (a) to Peter; (b) to the Twelve: (c) to 500 brethren, the majority of whom, Paul says, were still alive in A.D. 55; (d) to James; and (e) to all the apostles.

Leaving Mark out of account for the moment, we find that the other three evangelists all bear testimony to the empty tomb and to the Risen Lord.

Matthew (28) records (a) an appearance of the Risen Lord to the women as they fled from the tomb; and (b) an appearance to the Eleven on a mountain in Galilee.

Luke (24) records three appearances: (a) to Cleopas and another on the road to Emmaus; (b) to Peter (24. 34); and (c) to the Eleven and others in Jerusalem.

John (20-21) records four appearances: (a) to Mary Magdalene in the Garden; (b) to ten disciples on the same Sunday in Jerusalem; (c) to ten disciples, plus Thomas, a week later; (d) to seven disciples by the Lake of Galilee.

Obviously it is hard, if not impossible, to weave all this evidence into one consistent account. Let us admit that there are discrepancies. Yet these discrepancies show at least that no harmonising instinct was allowed to obliterate them. Furthermore, let us remember that discrepancies in different records of the same event do not prove that the event did not occur. (There are serious discrepancies in the accounts of Waterloo as given by Wellington, Marshal Ney, and Napoleon; yet no one dreams of denying that there was a battle of Waterloo.)

A study of all this evidence shows an agreement on two main points:

(1) The tomb was empty.

(2) Jesus appeared to his disciples on several occasions.

A well-known difficulty is the scene of the Resurrection appearances. Matthew and John (21) locate them in Galilee, whereas Luke and John (20) locate them in Jerusalem. But these divergencies need not trouble a Christian believer. If it be accepted that Jesus rose from the dead, it was as easy for him to manifest himself in Jerusalem and in Galilee as in Jerusalem only or Galilee only.

How then are we to interpret this evidence? The first of the well-attested facts is the empty tomb. It is there we must begin. The body of Jesus had somehow disappeared from Joseph's rock tomb. The theory that the body was stolen or hidden is frankly incredible. Had the Romans or Jews removed the body from the grave, it would have been an easy matter for them to refute the Christian claim by simply producing the body. We may be sure that they did not because they could not. On the other hand, to suppose that the disciples themselves hid the body and then went forth to preach what they knew to be a lie, passes belief. This would be to brand the disciples as impostors, and even a Jew like Klausner pronounces this incredible.

If, then, we accept the fact of the empty tomb, we may choose one of two explanations. First, we may believe that the physical body of Jesus was resuscitated, and that in that body he manifested himself to his disciples. Odd bits of evidence might confirm this view (see, for example, Luke 24. 36-43). But on this view it becomes no easy matter finally to dispose of the body of Jesus. Luke tries to dispose of it by translating it to the sky (Acts 1. 9). But such a view will not commend itself to the modern man. A physical body has no place in the spiritual world (cf. 1 Cor. 15. 50), and translation into the sky is not, for our thinking, the equivalent of passing from the mundane to the spiritual world.

Therefore, second, it is best to follow St. Paul and St. John in believing that the physical body of our Lord was changed into a spiritual one. With such a view the evidence of St. John (undisturbed grave-clothes, the ability of the Risen Lord to pass through closed doors) agrees well. And it is certain that this was Paul's view. In 1 Cor. 15 Paul declares that a change from a 'natural' body to a 'spiritual' body is the appointed destiny of Christian believers, and since he speaks of Christ as the 'first-fruits of them that sleep', he obviously believed the same wonderful change to have taken place in Christ's body. In his own phrase, the body of humiliation had become the body of glory. (Even a sceptic like Lake admits this.)

There we may wisely leave the matter. For the chief thing in the Resurrection narratives is the disciples' invincible certainty that their Lord had conquered death. Only on the basis of this belief can we explain the change that came over the disciples: before the Resurrection, like frightened sheep;

after it, as bold as lions. And only so can we explain the
conviction of living fellowship with a living Lord, which has
been the very nerve of Christianity for well-nigh 2,000 years.

There are three great witnesses to the reality of the Resurrection.

(1) The existence of the Christian Church. Had the Crucifixion ended the story of Jesus, there would have been no
Church.

(2) The existence of the New Testament. Who would have
troubled to write these documents if Jesus had ended his
career as a crucified revolutionary?

(3) The Lord's Day. No Christian Jew would have
changed the sacred day from Saturday to Sunday except for
the reason which the Christian tradition gives—that on this
day Jesus rose from the dead.

H. G. Wells once declared that the story of the Resurrection always reminded him of the happy endings that editors
and dramatists tacked on to essentially tragic novels and
plays. This is not the New Testament view. For the New
Testament writers the story of Jesus is not a tragedy which
must at all costs be turned into something glorious. Nor do
they see the Cross as a simple tragedy. It was part of their
Good News from the beginning (1 Cor. 15. 3). But then, for
them, the Cross did not stand alone. Always they saw it
along with the Resurrection as two aspects of one great
redeeming act of God. They did not see the Resurrection as
simply an illustration of survival: they saw it as a victory
uniquely won, and won in order that men might share in its
virtue. 'As in Adam all die, so in Christ shall all be made
alive.' 'Because I live, ye shall live also.'

Moreover the Resurrection was not an end but only a
beginning. 'All that Jesus *began* to do and to teach,' says
Luke, referring to all that led up to Jesus' exaltation. For
with the Resurrection the Reign of God came 'with power'
(cf. Mark 9. 1), the Holy Spirit was given, and Jesus became
the living and exalted one who incarnated, and still incar-
nates, himself in uncounted multitudes of his followers, so
that it may be truly said that 'the Gospels are not four, but

ten thousand times ten thousand, and thousands of thousands, and the last word of every one of them is ''Lo, I am with you alway, even unto the end of the world''.''[1]

[1] T. R. Glover, *Conflict of Religions in the Early Roman Empire*, p. 140.